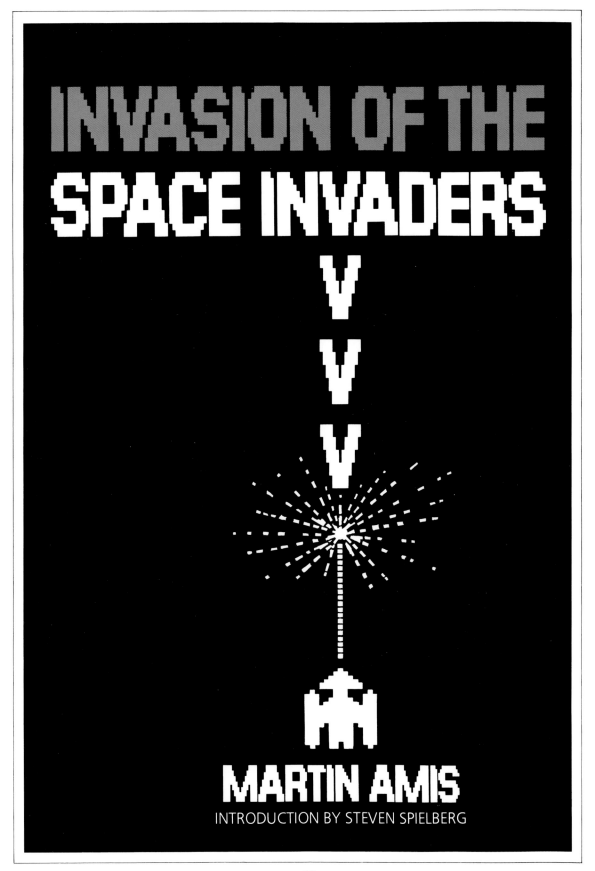

INVASION OF THE
SPACE INVADERS

MARTIN AMIS

INTRODUCTION BY STEVEN SPIELBERG

JONATHAN CAPE
LONDON

1 3 5 7 9 10 8 6 4 2

Jonathan Cape, an imprint of Vintage Publishing,
20 Vauxhall Bridge Road,
London SW1V 2SA

Jonathan Cape is part of the Penguin Random House group of companies
whose addresses can be found at global.penguinrandomhouse.com.

First published by Hutchinson in 1982
Published by Jonathan Cape in 2018

penguin.co.uk/vintage

A CIP catalogue record for this book is available from the British Library

ISBN 9781787331198

Printed and bound in India by Replika Press Pvt Ltd

Penguin Random House is committed to a sustainable future
for our business, our readers and our planet.
This book is made from Forest Stewardship Council® certified paper.

CONTENTS

The aliens have landed, and the world can never be the same again. You've got to believe it – there's a war on, and the strange thing about *this* war is that if you should once make the mistake of volunteering, you'll find active service hopelessly habit-forming.

Look at Martin Amis, the author of this book: once a fine, upstanding young man leading a blameless life, he was transformed within a few short games into a terminal case of video-addiction, his brain seething with little green monsters, lemons, smart bombs, boulders and fatboys – the tireless assailants of the video screen. Urgent treatment was called for, and now, after thousands upon thousands of games, to say nothing of the chastening experience of writing this book, the patient seems to be on the road to recovery.

But don't fall into the same trap: read this book and learn from young Martin's horrific odyssey round the world's arcades before you too become a video-junkie. Don't assume that, because of your innate strength of character, you can avoid this fate: it has happened to the best of us, and I speak as one who knows. I have actually exceeded 500,000 at Missile Command but have not broken beyond 75,000 at the super-updated machines.

The warnings are clear... Part I explains how the Invaders took over, virtually without anyone realizing what was happening, and infiltrated themselves into every corner of the known world, claiming victims of every race, colour and creed. Then, in Part II, you have your own consumer guide to the arcade machines, with advice on battle tactics from a seasoned campaigner (see above). Part III reveals how the Invaders, far from confining their activities to public places and consenting adults, have established themselves in our homes in various shapes and forms, to the extent that there's really nowhere left to go to avoid them.

Well – that's if you really want to. I don't want to be accused of collaboration, but some of them are really quite friendly when you get to know them...

Steven Spielberg

HALL OF MIRRORS: FUTURISTIC VIDEO PARLOUR IN MASSACHUSETTS.

PART 1

THEY CAME FROM OUTER SPACE:
THE VIDEO INVASION

Suddenly, it seems, this particular planet is under new management. In Earthling pubs, bars, motorway rest-stops, kebab houses, record marts, in Texan airports, Bengali hotel lobbies, Scandinavian eros centres, in Parisian nightclubs, on Greenwich Village street corners, in ice-cream

parlours, dentists' waiting-rooms, uni-sexual boutiques – and in the trans-global amusement arcades where pallid addicts loiter and dangle like mutated bats – you can behold the fizz and flash of a million close encounters, a million star wars. Invasion of the Body-Snatchers, Night of the Living Dead, They Came from Outer Space: it's all happening before our eyes.

The casualty wards of metropolitan hospitals are fighting an epidemic of colourful new maladies – Asteroid Elbow, PacMan Finger, Galaxian Spine, Centipede Disc. (God knows what this stuff is doing to our eyes.) Police stations maintain swelling dossiers on Space Invader-related crimes: in England, a little boy recently trousered his father's unemployment money *and* his granny's funeral fund to invest in several thousand games of Space Invaders at his local sweetshop. (The machines have also given the child-prostitution industry a fillip. Kids are coming

across for a couple of games of Astro Panic, or whatever. More about this later.) Sometimes the Invasion is nationwide, geopolitical: two years ago video-game fever caused a coin-shortage in Japan, where they have a lot of coins. Worldwide, the space-game racket turns over more money than films or records.

There appears to be no doubt about it. The Space Invaders have Invaded.

THE ALGEBRA OF NEED

What we are dealing with here is a global addiction. I mean, this might all turn out to be a bit of a *problem*. Let me adduce my own symptoms, withdrawals, dryouts, crack-ups, benders . . .

The habit might start with an innocent game or two at, say, a seaside arcade or an airport departure lounge. The experience is enjoyed and, perhaps, completely forgotten. For the time being, all is well. Then the Invadee discovers that the sinister machines lurk everywhere, infesting the neighbourhood pub or the lunchtime snackbar near the office . . . Frowning, smiling, you stroll over for a few games. You stroll over for a few games regularly. You give yourself a bit of extra time for the diversion. You hoard change. You start to encounter familiar, furtive faces in the queue to the machine. The murmured talk is all of Smart Bomb and Hyperspace, Fuel Count and Quadrant Warp.

'If you hit the saucer on the fifteenth shot, you score 300.'

'Spray your fire on the Pod and you get all the Swarmers.'

'Unless they bleed to another quadrant.'

'Saw a guy in here yesterday, he got 9,000 on his first life.'

'Wait till they go green, then dock the mother ship on the right.'

'Watch out. Here come the snowballs.'

'More thrust!'

'Narrow the angle!'

'Up!'

'Down!'

Gradually, the slang and code become intelligible. The weird, clandestine brotherhood seems to open up to let you in . . .

Before long, your evenings are punctuated by cautious excursions to the nearest video parlour. Seems all right in here too: someone on hand to give you change, reasonably friendly atmosphere, big reassuring bouncers. You go

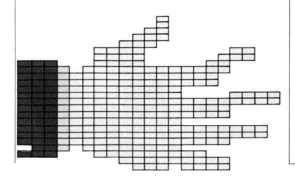

more and more often, finding (to your dismay and alarm) that you tend to break into a run over the last hundred yards. You start lying to your family and friends. 'Just going for a stroll' and 'Must post this letter' are the sort of things you hear yourself saying as you scurry through the door. (Oh, the shame and guilt. Oh, how you have to cringe and hide!) At night, the mind of the wretched Invadee is a cratered battlefield, buzzed by whining missiles, stalked by bristling aliens.

Your work starts to suffer. So does your health. So does your pocket. The lies increase in frequency and daring. Feelings of self-disgust assail you. Anyone who has ever tangled with a drink or drugs problem will know how the interior monologue goes. 'I think I've got this thing under control at last. It's perfectly okay so long as you do it in moderation. I was very good yesterday, and hardly played at all. So I had a long session this morning. Who's perfect? All right, I won't play tonight, just to show I can take it or leave it. But what's the big deal? Why take it so seriously? It's only a toy. A game or two won't hurt . . .'

The addict then indulges in a wild three-hour session. 'I'm never going to touch that stuff again,' he vows. 'That's it. I've had it. We're through.' Twenty minutes later he is hunched once more over the screen, giving it all his back and shoulder, wincing, gloating, his eyes lit by a galaxy of strife.

SUDDENLY ONE SUMMER

It happened in 1979. I was in the South of France — that summer, when the Invasion began.

I was sitting in a bar near the railway station in Toulon. I was drinking coffee and writing letters and generally minding my own business. The bar had a pinball machine, a creaking old hulk with a card-game *motif*. There were only a few locals in there at the time. Suddenly there was commotion, and the fat, aproned *maître* began to supervise a delivery at the door. Grunting heavies were wrestling with what looked like a sheeted refrigerator. They installed it in the corner, plugged it in, and drew back the veil. The Invasion of the Space Invaders had begun.

Now I had played quite a few bar machines in my time. I had driven toy cars, toy aeroplanes, toy submarines; I had shot toy cowboys, toy tanks, toy sharks. But I knew instantly that this was something different, something special. Cinematic melodrama blazing on the screen, infinite firing capacity, the beautiful responsiveness of the defending turret, the sting and pow of the missiles, the background pulse of the quickening heartbeat, the inexorable descent of the bomb-dumping monsters: my awesome task, to save Earth from destruction!

The bar closed at eleven o'clock that night. I was the last to leave, tired but content. The owner's wife smiled at me understandingly as I stumbled out. At first I thought it was just a holiday romance. But deep down I knew all along that this was the real thing. I had been ravished, transfigured, swept away. I had been Invaded.

Now, after nearly three years, the passion has not cooled. I don't see much of Space Invaders any more, it's true — though we're still good friends. These days I fool around with a whole harem of newer, brasher machines. When I get bored with one of them, a younger replacement is always available. (I still spend the odd night with Space Invaders, my first love — just for old times' sake.) The only trouble is, they take up all my time and all my money. And I can't seem to find any girlfriends.

VIDKIDS FIGHT IT OUT AT PENN STATION, NEW YORK. NOTE THE SHOULDER-WORK
AND BUTTOCK-HEFT THAT GO INTO BEING INVADED.

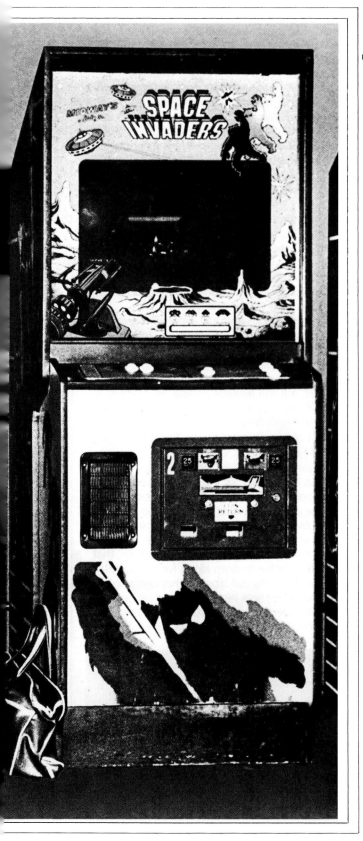

THE LAST WAVE

You think I exaggerate? I do, but only slightly. After all, the obsession/addiction factor is central to the games' success: you might even say that video-dependence is actually programmed into the computer. Illogical need is in the logic-board of each machine.

Nearly all the games operate on the principle of ascending difficulty and complication. 'You want to develop a healthy level of frustration,' states the vice-president of Atari (which gave us Asteroids). 'You want the player to say, "Gee, if I put another quarter in, I might do better".' Equally to the point, Atari might do better too. The longer the game goes on, the more spectacular the gimmicks become: new lights, new noises, new configurations from the heavens. As E. M. Forster said of the novel, the thing that impels you is the straightforward desire to know *what happens next*. Yes, oh dear me yes, the video game tells a story. The more money you put in, the better you get. The better you get, the longer the story lasts. And we all know how children feel about stories.

On one machine I know, the following words appear on the screen after the first wave of invaders has been dispatched: 'Well Done, Earthling. This Time You Win. Now Do Battle With Our Super Forces.' And suddenly, as a warning, the entire screen momentarily fills with the silver-green monsters. Oy! The Earthling reels back for an instant in sheer fright – and then starts to do battle with Wave 2. Wave 2 wipes him out. He feeds more money into the machine, wondering what Wave 3 will be like. The price of his curiosity is likely to be punitive.

While there is no known cure for the video-game habit, you *can* detoxify yourself of certain machines in the repertoire. Take my own experience with Space Invaders itself. It took thirty or forty games before I could destroy the first wave – or 'sheet' – of enemy aliens. The second wave starts lower down the screen, nearer your defences, and drops more bombs on you – and so on, until the fourth wave is an inch from your defending turret. Each wave cost me a further fiver, until I was confronted by Wave 9. A period of fanatical dedication and startling expenditure followed: and I wasted Wave 9 . . . Then, guess what? The Invaders retreat, right back to Wave 2, and the whole process starts again.

Hence this game (like most of the others) is theoretically infinite. All those stories that

circulate in the parlours – scores of five million or more, some kid playing for 52 hours on one 25-cent piece – suddenly take on credibility. We live in an age, after all, when people will make the most life-wrecking sacrifices for a dismissive footnote in the *Guinness Book of Records*. Having beaten the machine once, though, *my* affair with Space Invaders was as good as over. I never mess around with infinity, and I don't have the competitive fervour, or the energy, or the time, or the money, to try for those heights. No, from that day on, Space Invaders and I were through. I knew it. Space Invaders knew it. It was a big relief, I don't mind telling you. Within hours I had put all that behind me and was on to something completely different: Space Invaders Part II.

BUG-EYED MONSTERS

Who are these that haunt the electronic grottoes, where the machines sing and the Earthlings play? Who are these proletarian triffids, these darkness-worshippers, hooked on the radar, rumble and wow of friendly robots who play with you if you pay them to? You think those ogres and hellhounds up on the screens look pretty bad. But take a look around here, at the human aliens, and what do you see?

The strolling bouncers and extras in their damson djs, the sleepy-looking outlaw behind the glass screen with his money-bags and coin-chutes. Zonked glueys, swearing skinheads with childish faces full of ageless evil, mohican punks sporting scalplocks in violet verticals and a nappy-pin through the nose. Seven-foot black kids on roller-skates, coolly monitored by their more mystical and whacked-out older brothers, all gone on ganja, dreadlocks, and petty crime. Ten-year-old trogs, knowing little vandals, foul-mouthed and furious and very easily

frustrated (no one ever told them that you *mustn't be cruel* to defenceless machines). Queasy spivs, living out a teen-dream movie with faggot overtones. Bemused, doddering hippies, attracted by the lights; blazered schoolboys, fascinated, terrified, calling everyone Sir; classic, textbook child-molesters; and – in New York – hip Madison Avenue ad-execs and MIT whizzkids, enjoying their coked-up coffee break. These are the displaced mineshaft spirits of the present age – their grandparents must have worked underground. What are they all doing? How can they all afford it? *I* can't.

'The arcades are addictive,' says New York psychologist Mitchell Robin. 'The lights, the sound – that all makes it womblike.' You wonder: what kind of womb did this guy grow up in? In my view, most of the video parlours are – as venues, as places to hang out – no more addictive than Cockroach Motel. Dry heat crackling with smoke and spores, used junk-drink cartons and half-eaten wallyburgers, the less than glittering clientele. It's true that some American parlours are as clean and bright as kitchen-appliance showrooms (in the Pan Am games room at JFK, for instance, you can't even smoke); but the average arcade, let's face it, is like a Wimpy Bar in Hell. It's the *machines* that do all the addicting.

Lot's o' Fun, Family Leisure, Teddy Bear, One Step Beyond, Jesters, Golden Goose, Playland: these joints, some of which are 24-hour, have obvious attractions for the unemployed teenager, the hookey-playing schoolboy, or anyone else with a couple of hours to kill. They have obvious attractions too for the amateur urban anthropologist, as we shall see. But it is in spite of the arcades, not because of them, that the video-junkie trudges along for his fix. The true purist wants out from all that cacophony and sweat. He sees himself alone, cocooned, up on some spectral tower, just him and the game – fingers, controls, the writhing screen.

OPPOSITE, TOP AND BOTTOM RIGHT: CLEAN-CUT VIDKIDS WORK ON IMPROVING
THEIR SPATIAL AWARENESS
OPPOSITE, BOTTOM LEFT: PLAYLAND – THE BEST-RUN ARCADE IN TIMES SQUARE

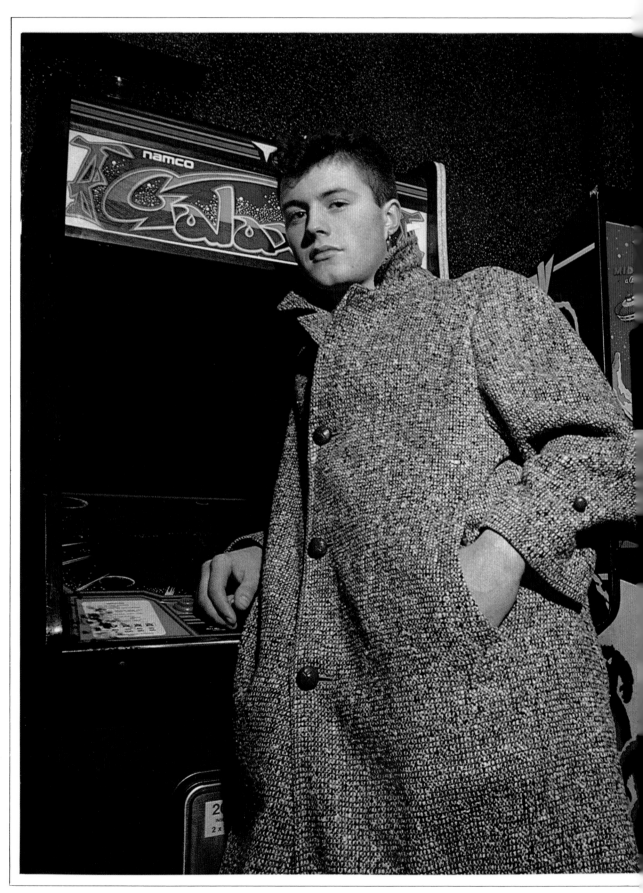

TYPICAL DEFENDERS OF THE PLANET: NOTE SYMPTOMS OF BATTLE FATIGUE.

THE GAME OF THE NAME

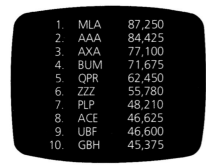

1.	MLA	87,250
2.	AAA	84,425
3.	AXA	77,100
4.	BUM	71,675
5.	QPR	62,450
6.	ZZZ	55,780
7.	PLP	48,210
8.	ACE	46,625
9.	UBF	46,600
10.	GBH	45,375

This is an imaginary but typical print-out for the end-of-day Top Ten. Most machines feature a gimmick of this kind: initials are achieved by rotating through the alphabet, backwards or forwards, then punching out the letters you require, using the normal play buttons. To appear on the Great Score sheet is a powerful incentive in space-game praxis – a yearning perhaps connected with schooldays and the honour or notoriety of having your name chalked up on the board, white on black. On some games, notably Space Invaders Part II, you get to put your full name on day-long display (provided no one tops your score): it flashes at the top of the screen in alternation with your record tally. Unsurprisingly, this latitude provides an obvious incitement to obscenity – obscenity in neon, too, which makes it all the more irresistible. Instead of seeing KEITH RAINE or NORMAN REID or whoever up there on the honoured line, you are more likely to be confronted by FUCK OFF or UP YOURS or SCUMBAG – or BALLOCKS, in a wide variety of spellings. If you ever see the word TAITO flashing away up there, incidentally, it isn't the name of some Japanese vidkid but the logo of the manufacturers.

There isn't much the dirty-minded graffitist can do with three letters, though of course you get many a COQ and FUC, and all the other configurations that don't appear on car number-plates, like YID and SOD and NIG. BUM, number four on the list above, is by far the most popular. But let's go through them one by one.

MLA, at least, is an honest and genuine initial (I would like to be able to say that Trouble is my middle name; unfortunately, though, my middle name is Louis). Number two, AAA, is the 'cool' thing to mark up, for the simple reason that it requires least effort (three brisk taps on the Fire button), showing the punter's contempt for the whole convention. Number three, AXA, which is also easy to type, refers to the Amazonian heroine of a cartoon strip which appears daily in the *Sun*: wandering through a contaminated, post-cataclysmic world, the statuesque Axa has various adventures which keep involving the loss of her clothes. BUM we have already dealt with. QPR, number five, stands for Queen's Park Rangers, the erratic second-division football team originating from Shepherd's Bush. ZZZ is a quickly attainable variant of AAA, with the added bonus of representing soporific boredom as well as disdain. Number seven, PLP, looks genuine to me, though of course it might be an erudite reference to the Parliamentary Labour Party. ACE is a self-admiring salute with the advantage, again, of being no trouble to mark up. UBF probably refers to the reggae-ish, multi-racial rock group UB40 (it might be a genuine initial, though I can't think there are many denizens of arcade-land with names like Ursula and Ugo). Number ten, GBH, stands, of course, for Grievous Bodily Harm.

THE ASTEROIDS DE LUXE TOP TEN: NOTE THE EXCELLENT GRAPHICS AND IMAGINATIVE THREE-LETTER ATTRIBUTION.

OPPOSITE: WORLDWIDE, FEARLESS DEFENDERS ARE AT THE FRONT LINE: HOW LONG CAN EARTH HOLD OUT?

FLAY IT AGAIN

Talking of Grievous Bodily Harm . . . There used to be an arcade near where I live called Play It Again Sam. I tended to look in there, oh, not more than four or five times a day. On many occasions I had to abandon a promising intergalactic battle – or lose concentration to a disastrous extent – as a far more tangible brawl took place a few feet from my back. One tried to keep playing until the last possible moment, but when ashtrays and billiard balls started humming past one's ears – well, it was usually time, I reckoned, to warp to another quadrant. You joined the other grumbling video artists out on the street, and waited for the technical hitch to be dealt with.

Sam's was 24-hour. One night, about 1 am, I was in there, quietly defending Earth as usual, when four policemen strode into the hall. Ten seconds later, Star Wars was underway – and not on the video screens. I myself was on Wave 9, with three ships and two Smart Bombs at my disposal, all set for a record score, and generally very reluctant to leave. In between skirmishes, I glanced to my left: two white youths were in the process of being apprehended; they were cartwheeling about in an explosion of up-ended pintables, swaying hot-drinks machines, and a blizzard of missiles from the sympathizers further back. I glanced to my right, towards the street. It looked like the 87th Precinct out there – Pandas, paddy-wagons, thirty or forty cops, a dozen nervous Alsatians. In they came. A policeman standing directly behind me stopped a glass ashtray with the back of his neck. I warped out.

On the street the boys in blue herded, threatened and pacified the disgruntled evacuees. Eventually the two youths were dragged out and crammed into the wagon, there to receive an elaborate roughing up, if the hi-fidelity sound effects were anything to go by. Sam's was barred up for the night. There was an outcry on the street. 'I had four lives left!' 'One more wave and I would have made Space Colonel!' 'What about my three credits?' 'I was carrying my last humanoid!' Peering inside, we could see the attendants cheerfully tucking into the free machines. They smiled and shrugged. There was nothing they could do.

The next morning I strolled into Sam's and asked one of these purple-suited stewards, a gentle, slow-talking Barbadian, what last night's rumble had been about. A Space Invaders-related crime? Had these guys committed murder for a few games of Frogger? 'Stolen property,' said the steward. 'Receiving. Ah, but then,' he drawled, 'they resisted arrest.' 'I know,' I said, 'I was in here.' That was certainly true: they had resisted arrest all right. The phrase had never meant much to me until that night. Boy, did those guys resist arrest.

Theft, pimping, drugs, GBH – all have been associated with the shadowy world of the space-game parlours. It is undeniable that such places are the scene of many a bundle, handbag snatch, wallet lift, and so on. Undeniable, too, that the Soho joints and their big-city equivalents contain their fair share of genuine desperadoes. But it is largely a matter of coincidence: all-night places attract all-night people. There is nothing inherently clandestine about the average parlour addict. These adepts of wipe-out and smart bomb, these dealers in death and destruction, these guerrillas of Space Fury, Berzerk and Astro Blaster, are really pretty gentle types.

Shortly after the night when all that arrest-resisting came down, Sam's was obliged by the Council to close its doors at 1 am. Shortly after that, at midnight. There were complaints, there were worried parents. Then one morning I came round the corner as usual, trying not to break into a run at the thought of Defender and Missile Command, expectantly fondling my 50-pence piece – and the rotating lights above Sam's entrance had ceased to flash. With faltering steps I approached the dark window. I stared in. All dismal and dead. The row of pinball tables, normally a raft of active colour, stretched away inertly into the gloom. The silent space games were shoved brutally into the corner. They huddled together resentfully, already looking neglected, ruined, scrapped . . . *I* couldn't repel or defeat those aliens, those avengers, those space intruders. In the end, the City Council had to go and do it for me.

BLEEPING SICKNESS

In the summer of 1980, the town elders of Snellville, Georgia, evicted all the video games from Gwinnett Shopette. 'Kids don't know when to stop,' said councilman S. W. Odum. Nor did the kids learn; they simply started cycling into the next county, in search of the Wizard of Wor. A year later, the Philippines slapped a ban on the space games, claiming that the machines were 'playing havoc' with the morals of their youngsters. No doubt the kids are now snorkling to Borneo to try their luck.

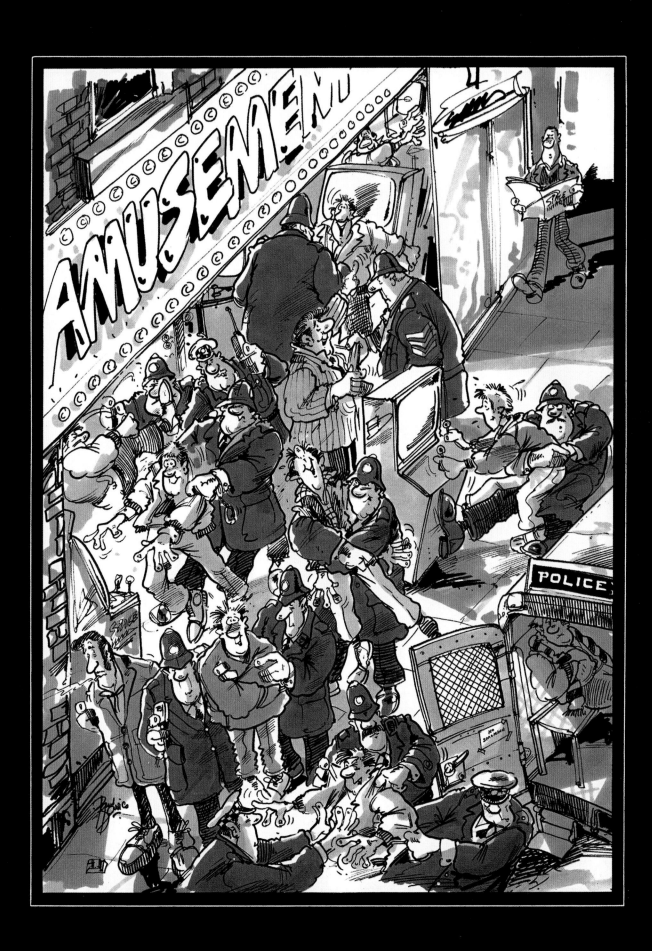

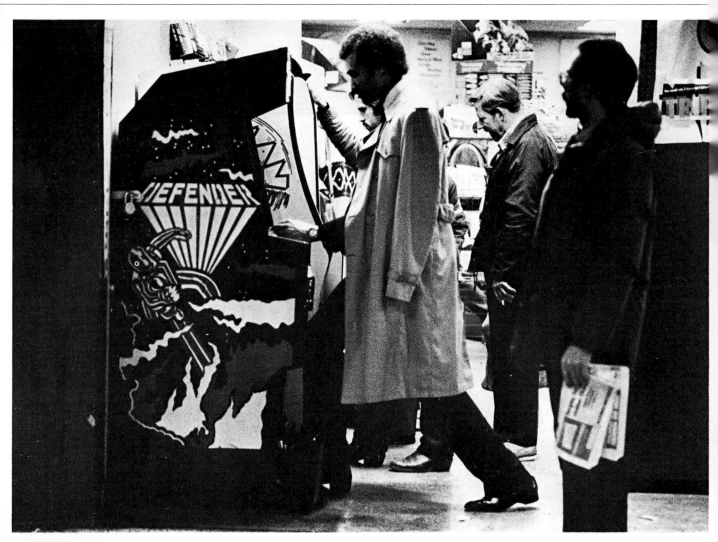

In Japan, soon after video fever broke, a 12-year-old boy held up a bank with a shotgun. He didn't want notes – just coins. Under interrogation, the kid cracked: it was Space Invaders that had put the squeeze on him. In Italy, where ordinary fruit-machines are banned, there have been many confirmed cases of Invaders-related child prostitution. England, 13 November 1981: it was reported in the press that a schoolboy, fourteen years old, had sold sex in a carpark for £2 – or, as he explained, for 10 games of Space Invaders.

'I guarantee it will become a problem,' says a spokesman of the American chapter of Gamblers Anonymous. Granted, the video games are addictive; but what exactly do they addict you to, apart from more video games? The speculative answers would seem to be these: violence, the kill-or-be-killed ethos, instant gratification, misanthropy, game-fixation, unreality. 'The more you can titillate your emotions, the less tolerant and patient you are going to be for things that don't deliver as fast,' says a professor of communications at the University of Southern California.

If you ask around the arcades, or just keep your ears open, the kind of fascination which the machines exert soon becomes clear. The key word is – adrenalin. The vivid melodrama of these games doesn't just involve and absorb the player: it makes him sweat and pant. With his lips thinning and his eyes bulging, he seems to take it all very *personally*. Also, the games could be a lot more violent than they are without quenching the large, and largely blameless, thirst that all children have for guns, blood, war, and so on. Kids are deeply competitive, they like noises, colours, gimmicks – they like games. But Ludo and Cluedo don't give them the physical and imaginative charge, this sense of fierce participation. The average arcade-fodder *homo* may not be very *sapiens* but, my, is he *ludens*. And games have simply never been as good as this before. One way or another, they burrow deep into the mind.

'When you first start playing, you can't get to sleep at all,' says Stephen Bradley, an 11-year-old Space Invaders champene who dispatched 64 sheets of green aliens at a sponsored contest in London last year. 'I used to lie awake hearing *bleep bleep bleep chug* all night, and seeing them dropping on me with my eyes shut. It got very painful in the head, but I grew out of it . . . If I get it now, I take a dose of cough medicine to knock me out.'

Young Stephen, of course, had made the mistake of inviting the Invaders into his own home, in the form of video cartridges. His father, a prosperous businessman, confessed: 'When we got Space Invaders at Christmas we were all at it, morning, noon and night. So I made a rule – no morning play, and nothing at weekends until the work is done.'

Sounds familiar, doesn't it? It's the sort of talk you hear from the 'reformed' alky, as he braces himself to describe his latest relapse. Mr Bradley, it seems, managed to master his obsession, and went on to resume a healthy and active life. Others, as they say, are not so lucky.

NO HIDING PLACE

Take the case of Anthony Hills – one of the more spectacular casualties of bleeping sickness. Seventeen years old, unemployed, heavily in debt and with all his possessions pawned, Anthony approached an old clergyman of his acquaintance, and asked for money. The verger, who was 74, had at some stage had sexual relations with this boy. He gave him £50 to stay quiet. He gave him another £50, and another. Soon his life-savings were gone. He started selling off his belongings. In utmost distress, he stole £300 from his church in the East End of London. Only after he had tried to commit

ABOVE: FUTURE SPACE CADET RELAXING BETWEEN STAR BATTLES AT PENN STATION.
OPPOSITE, TOP: FAVOURED LEG STANCE FOR DEFENDING.
OPPOSITE, BELOW: PACMAN AND ASTEROIDS CLASS AT MOUNT HOLYOKE COLLEGE, MASSACHUSETTS.

29

suicide did the verger eventually call in the law. 'All the money went on Space Invaders,' said Anthony as they took him away. He stood trial at the Old Bailey, and got four-and-a-half years.

One mother described her son as undergoing 'Jekyll and Hyde' transformations when the sickness loomed. Another woman went out with an axe, vowing to chop up every machine she could find. 'I spent every penny I could get on Space Invaders,' said her 14-year-old son. 'Now I'm going to try hard to give them up.' Police in the Sedgemoor area of Somerset claimed that the Space Invader craze had 'doubled housebreaking figures' in their precinct. Two boys in Barnsley blackmailed a classmate for extra video money. In Glasgow, unable to wait for his turn on a pub machine, a man attacked the innocent player who was hogging the console. The fight spread to the street, where the original player karate-kicked his assailant through a window – back into the pub.

Last spring the Space Invaders scored a notable victory: in the House of Commons. The Right Hon. George Foulkes, Labour MP for South Ayrshire, has long campaigned against the Invaders. Determined to subject the aliens to the control of local authorities, Foulkes was full of scare stories about youngsters with 'glazed eyes', who went about the place 'almost hypnotized'. Opposing him in the House was the Right Hon. Michael Brown, Conservative MP for Brigg and Scunthorpe. Brown spoke soaringly on the Invaders' behalf, confessing himself 'an avid supporter' of the games. The debate centred on questions of ideology, with Brown claiming that Foulkes wanted to impose his 'socialist beliefs' on the pleasure-loving multitudes. The Invaders won, by 114 votes to

94. Later, Brown told reporters that he had stopped at a pub on his way to the House – for a pint, and a quick game of Space Invaders. All too clearly, Brown was one of Them.

ON THE GRAPEVINE

The arcades have their own kind of oral tradition. Video knowhow (in the form of tips, scams, computer dodges, and so on) spreads as invisibly and unstoppably as the dirty joke. Who was the dogged parlour-layabout who first discovered that the Saucer in Space Invaders gives 300 points on every fifteenth shot? Which inspired deadbeat hit upon the idea of Smart Bombing the Pod-clusters at the beginning of each wave in Defender? What grim lurker pioneered the tactic of *lurking* in Asteroids?

One imagines a more or less infinite saga of trial and error, as the vidkids try, try and try again to outsmart the smug and glistening machines. Watch them pit their wits. But in fact the knowhow is communally achieved. Why is it that Rubik's Cube can blind the average adult with rage and bloodlust after half-an-hour, whereas the dullest child can solve it in a minute, then offer to make you pretty patterns on the swivelling square? It is well established that children show far more video flair than their elders. Just as chess masters begin to wane at forty, just as philosophers tend to do all their creative work in their twenties, so the space-game specialist peaks at puberty. This is largely a question of co-ordination and reflexes, and also of the curious brand of glacial concentration which the youngster brings to bear. What does the adult think about when he plays Space Invaders? He thinks about life, about survival, about what the hell he's up to, playing Space Invaders at his age. The kid, on the other hand, thinks about nothing except the pulsing screen. He thinks Space Invaders. He dreams Space Invaders.

And, of course, he belongs to the think-tank comprised by his peers. This is where the breakthroughs are made, the logic boards rumbled, the computers cracked. Word of mouth, it seems, is our frontline defence against the encroaching alien hordes. We're told that children don't bother to go to school much any more. How can they? They're too busy playing Space Invaders. But when they do put in the odd appearance, you can be sure that the song remains the same. This is what the playground tom-toms are saying: Fuel Count, Quadrant Warp, Hyperspace.

OPPOSITE: ASTEROIDS CHAMPENE FLASHING HIS BADGES.

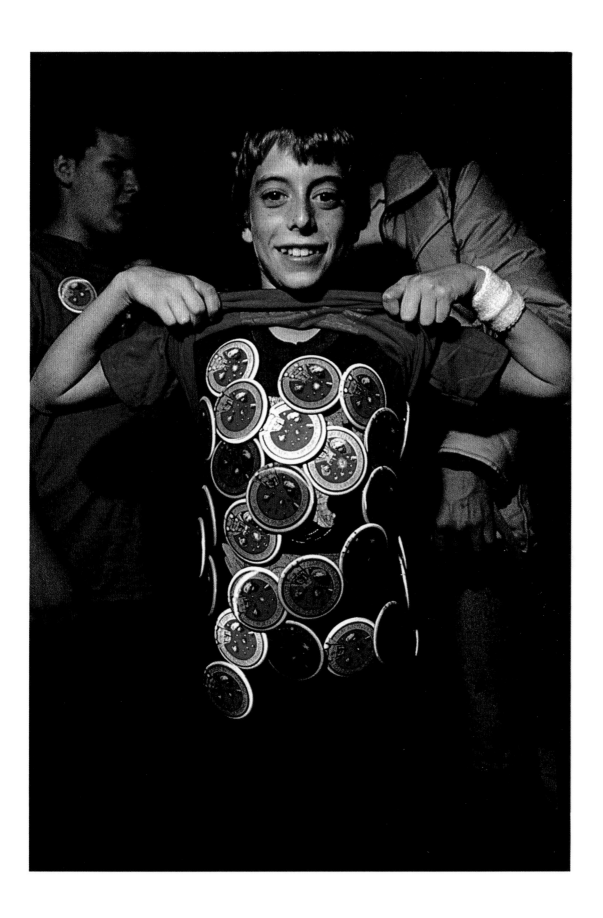

ATARI EXPERT WADING THROUGH ACRES OF CIRCUITRY BEFORE CRAMMING THE INFORMATION ON TO THE CHIP IN THE FOREGROUND.

CHIPS WITH EVERYTHING

Jack Stone, manager of the Magicraft Arcade in East London, noticed one day that his profits had suddenly dwindled. The machines seemed no less busy than usual. What was going on? After some careful observation he realized that the kids were using gadgets to spook the machines. By clicking electric cigarette lighters or battery-run kitchen gizmos near sensitive parts of the screen, the wizards of the arcades were screwing extra lives and extended plays out of the frazzled computers. 'When it comes to beating the system,' he said, 'every kid around here seems to be an electronic genius.'

Such incidents have been used to build up a rather laborious case in favour of the video games. You hear stories about altruistic, goody-goody Space Invaders, which have been used to help disturbed and handicapped children. You hear stories about brave, patriotic Space Invaders, which have been used to help crews of Nimrod submarine-hunter planes get better at detecting Soviet submarines. Some experts think that it is good for children to be good at Space Invaders, especially if they aren't good at anything else. 'This mastery experience is very important,' burbles Sherry Turkle of MIT. One of the most bizarre arguments put forward on the Invaders' behalf is that no video addict can afford to buy any drugs. He has spent all his money on Space Invaders instead. Yes, but the same could be said if he spent all his money on hand-grenades or ringside seats at bear-baiting bouts.

There are some Invader crusaders — educational consultants, and so on — who go even further. For them, the proud dawn of Space Invaders represents nothing less than an evolutionary breakthrough. 'We have a whole generation growing up who have no problem at all approaching the computer,' claims one Californian. In the new age of chip technology, 'they could become the haves'. So the vidkids will inherit the Earth! When you next see some ghoulish 10-year-old snarling and cursing over Mad Alien or Targ, remember that he isn't just having fun, killing time, wasting money: he's cultivating his computer literacy.

Of course, this argument does have some life in it. In America, computer indoctrination has long been a priority; nowadays there are computer summer-camps where children are sent to romp and gambol among the spools and printouts. It is true too, I suppose, that obsessive saturation in computer games might go hand in hand with a fleeting interest in computers *per se*. Some technological knowhow is bound to slip through, willy-nilly. We can see this stirring process at work even in the pages of the trade paper laughingly known as *Coin Slot International*. A more parochial and business-minded little gazette would be hard to imagine, with lead stories on Bingo tax laws and headlines like BRIAN CRIBBENS TO LEAVE CROMPTON GROUP on its front page. But even here the op.-ed. 'Quiz of the Month' feature includes questions such as 'What has to happen to the grid-cathode bias to increase the light output from the screen?' Well, do *you* know what has to happen to the grid-cathode bias?

All these pleas and provisos, however, are really by the way. The Great Invader Controversy, like so much else, is in the end a question of money. When the eggheads in Tokyo and Los Angeles roll up their sleeves and settle down over the logic boards, they aren't out to improve the punter's trigonometry or hand-eye co-ordination. They're out to get his money into the international coin slot.

OPPOSITE: DESIGNING THE CIRCUIT FOR THE WONDER CHIP BEHIND THE ATARI MACHINE

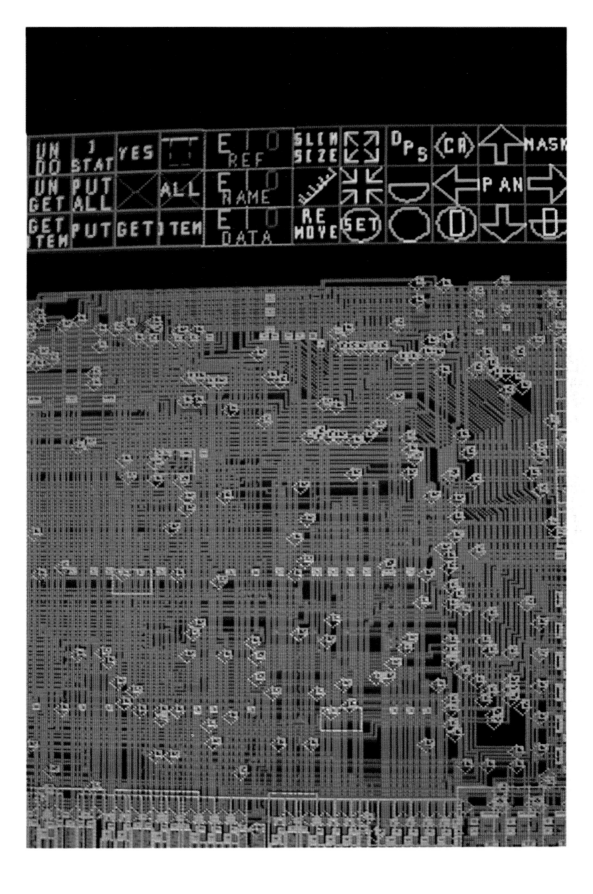

TELEVISION BREAK-OUT

D o you remember pub ping-pong, the
TV game where your little televisual bat
hit a little televisual ball until it had
dismantled the wall of white bricks at
the crest of the screen? It was an
intensely irritating game, and one that had
obsolescence written all over it. When they
heard its repeated *ping*, pub oldsters used to
look up from their shove-ha'penny and the
spotted bones of the dominoes, wondering how
long this moronic fad would last. But out of that
humble larva the monstrous regiment of Space
Invaders eventually grew.

Television Ping-Pong was the invention of
Nolan Bushnell. So was Television Tennis. So was
Television Football. So, in effect, was the
Television Game Compendium. At the time –
circa 1970 – Bushnell was an undergraduate at
the University of Utah. For his own amusement
he used to play space-theme games on the
computer in the engineering laboratory. Even
then he sensed the possibilities. 'But when you
divide 25 cents into an eight-million-dollar
computer,' he now explains, 'there ain't no
way.' He put the idea on the back-burner until
the technology developed and the price of
mini-computers shrank to manageable
proportions. Legend has it, among the glazed
Space Wanderers of the arcades, that Bushnell
devised the ping-pong games on the
work-bench of his father's garage, in true
crazy-scientist style. Actually, the pioneering
work all took place in his daughter's bedroom.

And the proto-game wasn't ping-pong: it was
a game which anticipated with astounding
precision the more elaborate video-consoles of
the future. Resembling a giant fibreglass parking
metre, it featured a rocket ship and a flying
saucer, complete with fire, thrust and turn
controls. It was called Computer Space. Only
2,000 were sold, and the idea once again
retreated while Bushnell went on to develop
Pong – a vast success. At the age of twenty-five
he sold his brainchildren outright for thirteen
million dollars. It doesn't exactly make you
weep, but subsequent events now indicate that
young Nolan was cruelly duped. The great man
has of course continued to prosper – these days
he works for the new robot-and-fast-food
venture, Pizza Time Theatre. However, it is
worth remembering that the video games
turned over five billion dollars last year. And
that's more than thirteen million dollars *per day*.

Throughout the 'seventies, TV Ping-Pong
diversified in a series of inconclusive splutters
and jolts. TV Break-Out provided a line of minor
innovations. The ball dismantled the wall; the
ball got trapped *behind* the wall, and danced
merrily about totting up points. Then the wall
descended! Then the bat got smaller! Pretty
desperate stuff – and of course none of this
fiddling could invest the dying novelty with new
life. On a different but parallel track, car games
of increasing sophistication were being
developed. Some worked on the principle of
straightforward verisimilitude (bucket-seat
booth, gears, an unravelling screen, high-speed
crashes, flags, oil-slicks, headlights). Others
exploited a more cerebral, labyrinthine appeal:
with joystick and accelerator, you had to zip
around the right-angled grid, avoiding one, then
two, then finally three 'enemy' cars, at
mounting speeds. The two rival attractions –
visual melodrama on the one hand, skilful
calculation on the other – cried out to be
synthesized. Then it happened.

It was in Japan, naturally, that the plans for
the Invasion were first formed. High up in the
spectral tower block of Taito Inc., teams of
computer experts and game psychologists
doodled and mused until, in 1978, they unveiled
that legendary screen: a squad of fat silver
insects, chugging its way down towards a lone
tank, which fires and then dodges back behind
the four green shields. Within months of the
Space Invaders' landing, no one in Japan could
use a public telephone or buy a subway ticket:
all the coins were nestling in the bellies of the
video games. Obviously the idea was a natural
for Japan – where (due to the sardine-can
overcrowding) everyone is always invading
everyone else's space. What fantasies of solitude
and freedom must have sizzled in front of those

LEFT: NOLAN BUSHNELL'S PROTOTYPE, COMPUTER SPACE, © 1972.
OPPOSITE, TOP: CENTIPEDE SPECIALISTS IRON OUT BUGS IN THE COMPUTER.
OPPOSITE, BELOW: CENTIPEDES BY THE HUNDRED, AWAITING ASSEMBLY.

screens! The big question was whether the appeal of the game was exportable. It was, and the rest is history – colonial history, in fact, as nation after nation throughout the earth kissed the sword of the little green men.

EXIT MONSTER MODE

Nowadays, in Silicone Valley, California, and its equivalents across the globe, morale is high, even idealistic. It is clear that these video factories are almost embarrassingly good fun to work at. As Kurt Vonnegut said of Cape Kennedy, there is a supercharged, erotic atmosphere in the funfairs of the new technology, and the employees are always having to play down the extent to which they enjoy their work. Play, work: these activities are normally opposed, but at such places they have plainly been cheerfully united. 'Multi monster sequence,' scribbles the worker. 'Every other wave: no friend. For each attack IF timer equals 4 THEN "too slow", exit monster mode. After monster is zapped, IF timer is 4 THEN reinitialize monster mode.' Whew! How long to go before lunch?

The hip young heroes of Atari, for instance, are convinced that they stand on the very brink of evolutionary breakthrough. The development of the video games is seen as roughly equivalent to mankind's slow crawl from the primal broth of creation. Any day now, it seems, *homo sapiens* will once more be towelling himself down on the fresh dunes of tomorrow. 'The computer,' says Atari's Steve Jobs, 'is one of the pinnacles of Western rational thought. They bring together physics, electronics, chemistry and mathematics; they bring logic, and

philosophy, information theory, all that. And the people working on these computers possess a passion about the discovery and creation of something. It's a passion that I have only seen matched in people pursuing what they consider to be the truth of their existence. It's the same purity of spirit I have experienced in monks.' So perhaps the foul-mouthed, grimacing trogs of the arcades aren't just improving their geometrical and spatial awareness: what they're really doing is searching for the meaning of life.

The laughter of fools, however, is like the crackling of weeds in the flower-pot. Jobs speaks wise words – in theory, anyway. Take the notion of teaching special relativity with video games. It is possible to program any set of physical laws into the 'microworld' of the customized TV screen. As was the case with the educational science-fiction stories of the mid-century, it is instructive to alter the ratios so that the laws are more noticeable than in everyday life. 'So on the screen,' says a physicist, 'you make the speed of light be ten miles an hour, put in some gravity, make it a game, and kids will start learning special relativity, the same way they learn to calculate parabolas without knowing what a parabola is, or what calculating is, in order to catch a baseball.' The game already exists, at MIT, and has been used with encouraging results.

Consider the following, a game of the future. I quote from an instructive article by Paul Trachtman in the *Smithsonian*:

You have a ten-year reign as a king and you have so much grain, so many people and so much land. You can buy or sell land for grain but you can't plant more acres than you have people to work at farming them. If you don't feed your people enough, they start to die. If they die, you can't plant as much grain anymore, and you may get into a downward spiral. But if you plant too much and store it, rats eat some of it . . .

And so on. If such a game were mass-produced and unleashed on the arcades, what would it be called? Malthus? The Social Contract? No, it would be called Ratter; it would have loony-tune rodents that winked at you between bites; it would have a farmer with a funfair hammer and a farmer's wife who jumped on a stool every time a rat squeaked; it would have a big grinning cat which scored a lump of cheese every time you . . . The predictions of the video eggheads are grand and stirring; at the time of writing, though, all the trends in the industry stubbornly point the other way.

Towards the end of 1980 it seemed that the space-game bonanza was finally levelling out.

OPPOSITE: A DAZZLING ARRAY OF GRAPHICS FROM THE MACHINE MAST-HEADS. JUST WAIT UNTIL YOU SEE THE SCREENS.

The dilettantes and casual punters had had their kicks and moved on to something else, whereas the addicts, the true bug-eyed monsters, were so well-attuned by now that they could play for hours on a single coin. (The owner of the One Step Beyond arcade in Arlington Heights, Illinois, kept his joint open all night while a fifteen-year-old notched up sixteen million points at Defender – all night, for 25 cents.) Profits were plummeting. Now was the time to launch a whole new strike force. What did the public get? The Pythagorean, Super Logarithm, Import Control, Logical Positivism Part II?

They got Frogger, Donkey Kong and Pro Golf. In an acquisitive panic, the video moguls decided to plump for the banal fantasies of the nursery, the cinema, and the grandstand. I venture to suggest that these games will not last. They will not last because they are boring games. But the fact remains that the video operators will always go where they think the money is, and will always be faddist in tendency. It is a question of economics – not kings and land and grain and workers, but money in the slot.

TAKE ME TO YOUR LEADER

What ingenuity, what wit, what clarity of thought – all to gratify the fickle vidkid! 'The technology used in those games is often more advanced than that used in America's weapon systems,' said an FBI spokesman last year. Silicone Valley was, apparently, five years ahead of the Pentagon. After the invasion of Afghanistan, President Carter forbade the export of high technology to the Soviets. Anxieties grew about 'technological transfer activities' in the toy industry, whereby technology was sold to a third party who promptly sold it to the Russians. In other words, the Space Invaders were sanctions-busting. The FBI got so worried that they sponsored a TV ad, fronted by that fine American Efrem Zimbalist Jr, to warn the nation of these dangers. This was a marvellous credibility-bid, since everyone who watches television knows that Efrem and the FBI are really the same thing ... But wait a minute. There's something about the squareness of Efrem's head. Are you sure he's not a robot, a cyborg, or at the very least an android? He certainly looks like a Space Invader to me.

General Donn Starry, who as his name suggests has long been beguiled by the video-game arcades, is the commander of

TRADOC, the US Army's Training and Doctrine Command. Under his orders the logic-board of the Atari tank game Battlezone was recently commandeered and adapted for military use. They added helicopters, allied tanks and personnel carriers. 'When we demonstrated the game at an armour conference at Fort Knox this spring,' said General Starry's aide, 'one of the generals who saw it said that we should have a fist come out and punch the guy in the head if he's stupid enough to fire at a friendly vehicle.' Atari promptly knocked up a $15,000 table-top tank game – the MK-60. Like any video game, it gets more difficult as the player prolongs the game.

'That seems to be the psychology behind Atari,' concluded one Major Robinson. 'You never can win, and you always can get better.'

Meanwhile, quite unaware of his contribution to the cold-war effort, the video-game distributor sits slumped in his office, morosely easing back a cuticle. Little does he ponder on the real battle zone, the real invasion. His Donkey Kongs and Froggers are out at their strategic soaksites, his PacMan-menders are skidding purposefully through the London streets; in the back rooms the boys toil, converting Galaxians into Defenders, refurbishing Missile Commands, unscrambling Scramblers. The telephone rings. 'No. No way. A Tempest maybe, a Pleiad probably, but an Asteroids? Forget it. Can't do a Defender. What about an Avenger? Or a Hustler? Or a Cresta?' The intercom buzzes. 'Yeah, all right. I know, I know. Tell him we'll get someone out there by opening time. Is Yukio free? He can do it.'

He releases the intercom button and swivels in his squeaky black-leather chair. 'Business is still strong,' he will tell you. 'It's not what it was last year, but it's still strong. Asteroids are still good. The De Luxe was a bit of a disappointment. The space games, they're fading. It's the Disney-type games they all like now. We've had Frogger out on a soak for a couple of weeks now. Brilliant. There's a lot of money around. Has to be. You know what I pay my repairmen? These days, when something goes wrong, it's not a bent coin stuck in the slot. It's the software not the hardware. You have to get the logic-board out.'

The telephone rings again. 'He wants a Space Invaders? What, a real, genuine, original Space Invaders? All this nostalgia. Some people ... they're just living in the past.'

In the back room, mechanics, engineers and computer geniuses are crooked over the eviscerated machines, busy with repairs, servicings and conversions. A young man sits playing with a dismantled Defender. He has the control console on his lap and the screen propped up on a bench a few feet away. At my request he puts the machine through its paces with negligent dexterity. For a while we talk about Mutant-avoidance, Swarmer-technique.

'It must be quite a job,' I said, 'playing Space Invaders all day.'

'Yeah,' he said with a grin.

'What do you do in the evenings?'

His face became serious, reflective, puzzled. 'Well, usually I just go out for a few games of Space Invaders.'

I checked with Security, then took the lift down to the main hall – a TV showroom of video-ware and new, split-level pintables. I went out the back way, through the storage areas. It was like a futuristic car-lot, a techno-dump: mad old Asteroids with frizzled wiring; *seppuku*-victim Galaxians trying to hold in their guts; blind, shot-faced Vulcans and Spectars; shoulder-to-shoulder Astrofighters, forming the soup-line into the shadows.

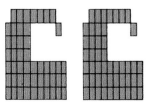

DON'T TALK THAT WAY

On the morning of New Year's Day, 1980, I entered a bar near the Panthéon, in Paris. This was a good bar, which as a sideline ran a roomful of pinball machines and embryonic video games. I was with a friend, a hard-drinking journalist, who had drunk roughly three times as much Calvados as I had drunk the night before. And I had drunk a lot of Calvados the night before. I called for coffee, croissants, juice; with a frown the barman also obeyed my friend's croaked request for a glass of Calvados.

Then we heard, from nowhere, a deep, guttural, Dalek-like voice which seemed to say: 'Heed! Gorgar! Heed! Gorgar . . . speaks! *Gorgar*!'

'. . . Now what the hell was *that*?' asked my friend.

'I think it was one of the machines,' I said, rising in wonder.

'I've had it,' said my friend with finality. 'I can't cope with this,' he explained as he stumbled from the bar.

I approached the line of pintables. Sure enough, there was a new machine, called Gorgar. As depicted in the graphics, Gorgar was a mean, cyclopic character with horns and animal fangs. Cautiously, I put a franc into the slot – and Gorgar went ahead with his act. Such was my awe and terror that the game was over in a few seconds, at which point Gorgar remarked, 'Gorgar! Heed! He – got – you! *Gorgar*!' Naturally I put in another franc, and fast. 'Heed! Gorgar! Gorgar . . . speaks!' At the end of the game Gorgar cleared his throat to announce that he, Gorgar, had got me again. But in mid-Gorgar! his voice trailed off like a dying gramophone – Gorgaaaaaaar . . .

Gorgar was suffering from teething troubles: he had lost his voice. A guy came and fixed him that afternoon, or he tried. Gorgar, so vigorous and powerful in all other respects, had an awful lot of trouble with his voice that week. Whenever I see Gorgar these days – and there are still a lot of Gorgars about – there's always something wrong with him. Poor Gorgar. He never could seem to shake that throat trouble of his.

Now, of course, every third-rate video game on the market whines and gibbers at you everywhere you go. For some reason, vocalization appears to suit the routine growls of a pinball machine – Launch Mission!) Circuit Completed!) and my favourite, *Blackout!* – but there is something pretty fatuous about being told what's what by a glorified television. One machine tauntingly reminds the player that he 'eats coins'; another keeps saying 'Mordar, Mordar' in embarrassingly adolescent tones. In Playland, by far the best arcade in the Times Square area of New York (just as its namesake in Wardour Street is the pride of Soho), they have the best two Defenders I have ever played – beautifully exact and responsive. But can a guy Defend in peace? No, you are driven to murderous distraction by an adjacent game which, whether anyone is playing it or not, incessantly dares you to do battle with 'the greatest warrior in space' – and the voice is so hammily B-feature that it sounds, exasperatingly, like the greatest *lawyer* in space. Do You Dare Do Battle With The Greatest Lawyer in Space? Bag it! Go to hell! Shut up already! I know, oh I know that the video addict is an outcast, a leper; but we're not *that* lonely. We don't pay money for a bit of conversation. We have each other to talk to, after all. The talking-game gimmick none the less

OPPOSITE: THE SPACE INVADERS MOTIF SPREADS TO PINBALL; BUT THE INSPIRATION BEHIND THE MONSTER IS RIDLEY SCOTT'S *ALIEN*.

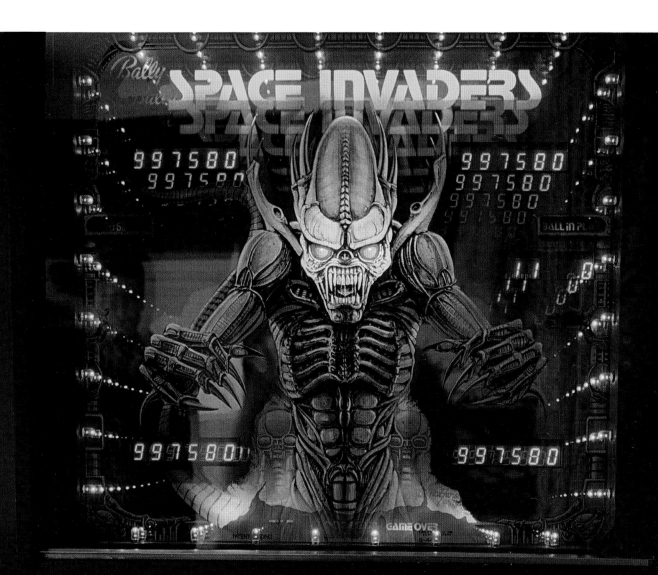

reflects a shrewd bit of psychologizing by the Atarians. In the age of the hand-held television, the Sony Walkman, how fitting that a video game should aspire to be the perfect companion. Why be lonely? For twenty pence you can shoot the breeze with a machine. Who needs anyone?

THE BLANK-SCREEN GENERATION

So in the electric arcades, with heads bowed and shoulders working, giving it all their bicep and buttock (their intent, terrified-seeming faces reflected in the screens) – the Triffids, the Invadees play on into the night. Where do they get the money? Having got the money, why don't they do something else with it? It doesn't take much of a sociological eye to see that these people aren't very gainfully employed, in any sense. Not many people in here look normal, well-adjusted and human, like me. (And anyway, I'm not just playing Space Invaders. I'm researching a book.) 'Got 20 pee, mister?' you get asked. For a coffee? For a warming bowl of broth? No: for another game of Astro Blaster.

These, then, are the punks, the blankies, the full generations of vandals and no-hopers we have been promised for so long. There is something wilful, is there not, something *voulu*, about putting the last coins you own into one of these squat monsters, already chockful of your wasted cash? Exactly so: but that is part of the spur. What more eloquent and effortless way of showing that you don't care, that nothing matters? You'd think that the 'eighties would be the least auspicious time for the birth of a vast and ravenous leisure industry. Supposedly we can hardly walk and breathe, with all this stagflation in the air. And yet everything you see contradicts such an impression. Money has never looked cheaper. It looks disposable, throwaway stuff.

There is much that is cheerless in watching the way these sub-teens busy themselves in the arcades. The impatience, the knowingness, the ever-ready anger and frustration, the sly nonchalance when things go well . . . For all I know, these are the Nobel Prize candidates of the 21st century. For all I know, such things as the Thalidomide tragedy are going to seem pretty minor when we find out what these things are really doing to us. For all I know, the whole debate will soon look as inconsequential, or as coincidental, as the heated controversies

about snooker and pool earlier in the century.

As Isaac Asimov has said, 'Kids like the computer because it plays back. You can play with it, but it is completely under your control. It's a pal, a friend, but it doesn't get mad, it doesn't say ''I won't play'', and it doesn't break the rules. What kid wouldn't want that?' There

is, I suppose, no real reason why you should, but if you wanted to locate space-game playing as a moral activity, one would have to align it with pornography and its solitary pleasures. As such, it is no worse than any other form of selfish and pointless gratification; it is also very appropriate to the age. One notes with weary satisfaction

that there is a new video game on the way called Softcore. Now what is *that* going to be like? You are the man. You have to gain access to the lady's bedroom, avoiding mother-in-law, angry husbands, etc. By using the Thrust button, you . . .

My own explanation for the space-game craze is as follows. It has to do with space and, of course, with games. We live in a time of extraterrestrial hopes and anxieties. I read a report somewhere that claimed that an incredibly high proportion of the population – something like one in three – believe that all their thoughts and actions are determined by creatures from another world. And these people aren't cranks, readers of the *National Inquirer*, fantasists who think that President Kennedy is alive and well, living with Buddy Holly on the planet Krypton. They are lawyers, truckers, things like that. An MP friend of mine assures me that most city councils have 'Martian Squads' in their utility and maintenance departments.

Apparently, a routine morning's work for the squad goes something like this:

'Good morning, madam. We've come about the Martians.'

'Thank God for that. About time. Well, they're up on the roof again.'

'Are they now? Right then! We'll soon sort *them* out.'

The squad goes up to the roof. They have a smoke and a chat and come back down again, dusting their palms.

'I don't think they'll be bothering you again, madam.'

'I certainly hope not.'

'How's the boiler?'

'All right, except sometimes it makes this funny noise . . .'

It would seem that many of us have vacant or dormant areas in our minds, empty spaces waiting for invasion. This is the area whose expansion leads to quirkiness, eccentricity, madness. It used to be the Devil who invaded these spaces in the common mind. Now, for obvious reasons, it is the Martians, the Space Invaders, who seek entry.

The other, uncomplicated thing about the space games is that they are wonderful *games*, having to do with nothing but themselves. They simply help to invade the empty spaces in life. Now, if you'll excuse me, I must put this aside and get down to something rather more serious. The Martians have been getting out of hand round my way lately. I must get down to HQ and resume my mission. I must get back to defending Earth.

PART 2

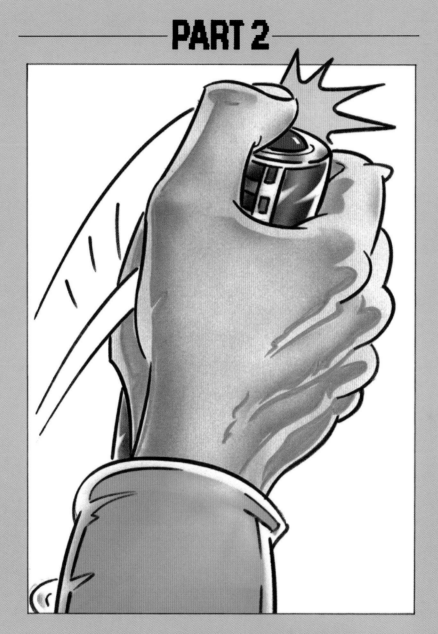

THE HOME FRONT:
THE ALIENS ARE HERE TO STAY

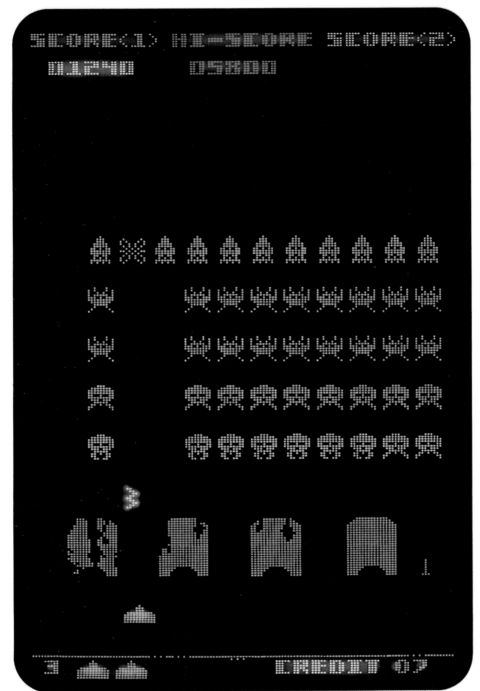

EARLY ON IN WAVE 2; TAKING OUT THE LEFT-HAND FILES.

Space Invaders is owed the respect paid to the senior member of any family – even though we all admit that the old boy has become a bit of a bore in his declining years. Now don't get me wrong. If it hadn't been for Space Invaders, none of us would be where we are today.

The main innovation of Space Invaders was as follows: *it gave you real drama on the screen.* Who cares whether you can eliminate dots with an electric tennis ball? So what if you can knock down ten plastic cowboys on a shooting range? Who gives a toss when a toy car skids on a patch of toy oil? After Space Invaders, we were *defending Earth*, against monsters, in sublunar skies. Here they come again. . . .

The tyro player, the kid to whom the experience of being Invaded is relatively novel, puts in his coin, slides his turreted tank into centre stage, and blasts happily away at the massed, bomb-dumping aliens. For thirty seconds or so he'll be pleased with his progress and confident about his chances. Thirty seconds later, all three of his tanks, or 'lives', will have been blown away.

Why? The phalanx of enemy invaders moves laterally across a grid not much wider than itself. When it reaches the edge of the grid, the whole army lowers a notch. Rule one: **narrow that phalanx**. Before you do anything else, take out at least three enemy columns either on the left-hand side or the right (for Waves 1 and 2, the left is recommended). Thereafter the aliens will take much longer to cross their grid and slip down another rung. Keep on working from the sides: you'll find that the invaders take forever to trudge and shuffle back and forth, and you can pick them off in your own sweet time.

The only remaining problem on Wave 1 is in taking out the last two or three aliens. Try to ignore, by the way, the pulsing, accelerating throb of the machine as the enemies descend, which is just meant to spook and panic you. The last two or three aliens move faster and spray off bombs at an angle. If they reach the surface, then the game is over, extra lives or no extra lives. It'll take you a few times out before you can start picking these guys off with any confidence. Advice: position your tank under the eave of a defensive barricade, **and keep your eye on the aliens, not on the bombs**. Got him? Now that Wave 1 is over – whew – let's move on to Wave 2. But first a word about Saucers.

'Do you *count*?' is a question that most Invadees ask each other pretty early on in their acquaintance. *Counting*, which bears resemblances to *Lurking* in Asteroids, is a tactic (despised by some) which relies on the predictability of the machine's logic board. The Saucer in Space Invaders, which bleeps across the top of the screen at fairly regular intervals, gives scores of 50, 100, 150 and 300, seemingly at random. Once, in Nice, I watched a master Invadee doing his stuff – and *every* Saucer gave him 300. 'Pourquoi?' I asked. Why the hell does that happen to him and hardly ever happen to me? The answer was, of course, that Monsieur

was a *counter* – and so was I from that day forth.

The Saucer's scoring pattern is linked to the number of shots you fire. In brief, the Saucer scores 300 on your 23rd shot and on every 15th shot thereafter. **Start counting**. I once overheard one Invadee tell another: 'Fire another three and go for 150 on the ninth.' No doubt there are more tricks and gimmicks of this kind, but in my view too much *counting* takes the fun out of being Invaded. (NB: don't hang around too long at the end of a Wave waiting for extra Saucers to show up. If you get below eight Invaders on the board, then you get no more Saucers anyway.) Some players don't bother with the Saucers at all. 'Listen,' they'll tell you. 'Screw the Saucers. My job is to defend Earth.'

The Second Wave, which starts off a rung lower, is dealt with in the same way as the First. Narrow the phalanx, work from the sides. In general, **let the Invaders move towards you**. Don't chase the body of aliens across the screen. Every game has a distinctive fire-and-dodge action that you will gradually master. In Defender it is a fast two-finger action on Fire and Thrust, in Asteroids a spray action on Fire and Rotate. In Space Invaders it is a continuous co-ordination of Fire and retreat, Fire and retreat. The Invaders edge sideways towards you; you peep into range, let off a shot, and retreat again – all fast and fluid, rising to about two shots a second in hectic play.

On the Third Wave your tactics change. The lowest invaders are now, at the outset, far too

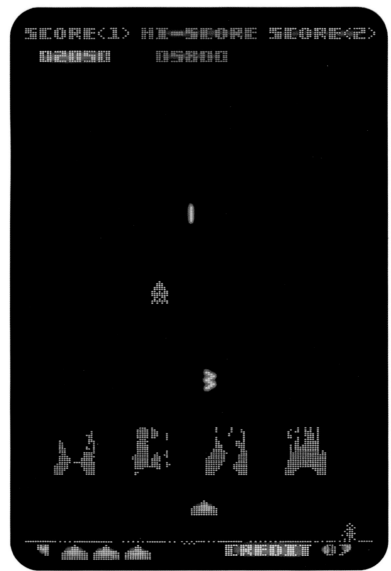

SCORE<1>   HI-SCORE   SCORE<2>
02050   05800

THE LAST OF THE GREEN MEN, MOVING FAST AND FIRING AT AN ANGLE.

low for comfort, and you can't expect to hang around on the left-hand side of the board while the rest of the aliens get even lower. (It's possible, though: I have seen this done right through to the sixth and seventh Waves, when the lowest Invaders start off a queasy green. But don't *you* try it.) Now your best bet is to jerk

across the screen, taking out at least six of the lowest rank, and position yourself beneath the last but one file on the right. Take out this file, then the file on its immediate left, then the file on the far right. Now you scoot back leftwards across the screen, blasting away as you go, and get to work on the left-hand side. This is your pattern from here on. After Wave 8 or 9 (machines vary), the screen gulps, swallows its pride, and goes back to Wave 2. I'm not saying it's easy. It cost me several thousand francs.

A footnote. It has not escaped the notice of some Invadees that when the aliens get down to the very lowest rung, the rung that precedes total destruction — they stop firing bombs. You can slide around underneath them, touching

ALL BARRICADES DESTROYED; SEMI-INVISIBLE SAUCER; INVADERS LIKELY TO BREAK INTO TWO.

them with your nozzle, and survive! Some Invadees have attempted to develop a play-strategy on this basis: they retain a lone alien at the top left-hand corner of the board, and allow the right-hand files to descend, then pick them off when they are bright green but bombless. Well, it is fun – and gives you an odd feeling of invulnerability, even of invisibility. But one slip and the game is over. And I ask you: is this any way to defend Earth?

SPACE INVADERS PART II, SUPER INVADERS, ETC., ETC.

After the success of the original machine, several mutant variations were quickly spawned. We saw – and battled with – amoebic invaders that split in two when hit; flashing phantom Saucers that dumped bombs, alien reinforcements,

barricade ballast; we saw the introduction of the highest-score nameplate, the gimmick whereby the day's most successful Invadee got to print out his name – or, more often, his favourite swear-word – at the head of the screen (see page 25). These variations made for many absorbing hours, tensed over that hot black screen. But none solved the original problem of Space Invaders Part I: the eventual boredom of the first two waves. Anyway, by that time, we were all playing Galaxian and Asteroids instead.

GALAXIAN

CONCORDE DESCENDING WITH FULL ESCORT.

Chronologically, Galaxian was the natural successor to Space Invaders. I remember the crowds that clustered round the spanking new machines in December 1979. That new whining noise! Invaders that curved down at you through the air! Two francs a pop, instead of one! This last innovation was no great incitement to play the new game; and for a long time my only feeling about Galaxian was that it had liberated the old Space Invader machines, which now cowered in the corners of the bars, spurned, ignored, and grateful for any playmate. But after a while I bowed to progress, along with everybody else.

Above your ship – or rather, above your Galaxhip – the new aliens hover like a congested aviary of exotic birds. The aviary shimmers back and forth across the top of the screen in a syncopated shuffle. Singly at first, then in pairs and trios and flocks, they begin to swoop down on you, firing little white bombs. Pretty soon, the player is faced with an intriguing if limited array of battle situations – stay in the corner or come out firing? dodge the blue bird or get under that red one? Just above the enemy aviary two or more alien ships – little yellow Concordes – wait their chance: when they descend they do so in a tight convoy, escorted by two red birds. The Concordes pay a variable point dividend, as much as 800 if you nail them *after* nailing their escorts. As in many space games, the rapidity-of-fire rule is as follows: **the instant that your bullet hits its target, a new bullet is available for fire.** Thus, if a Concorde and a red bird are immediately above your nozzle, two super-rapid shots will dispatch them both. This is the way to pick up those 800s. Once a Concorde is shot, **every flying bird on the screen stops firing bombs.** So zip around and pick a couple off.

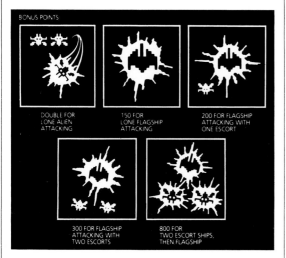

BONUS POINTS

DOUBLE FOR
LONE ALIEN
ATTACKING

150 FOR
LONE FLAGSHIP
ATTACKING

200 FOR FLAGSHIP
ATTACKING WITH
ONE ESCORT

300 FOR FLAGSHIP
ATTACKING WITH
TWO ESCORTS

800 FOR
TWO ESCORT SHIPS,
THEN FLAGSHIP

Galaxian may well be the only space game that doesn't get markedly more difficult as the battle proceeds. The birds swirl and whine a little more frequently, you might get as many as four Concordes per wave, but no new adversaries are introduced and the speed remains constant. Ho-hum . . . Between ourselves, it can be quite restful, playing Galaxian. The game is melodious, easy on the eye – a charming game. But a great game?

It is better, at any rate, than the hysterically souped-up variations which followed Galaxian on to the market. In some of these the Concorde swoops down with as many as eight or ten red birds in tow; in others the speed control has simply been turned up, to accelerate games (and cash-flow); in others the Galaxhip bombs can be wobbled and swerved by your joystick (this is an ingenious and utterly pointless modification); in yet others the humming birds have had their angles of fall tampered with and zip around in impossibly sharp curves, thereby reducing you to random fire (the sure sign of a rock-bottom game).

Now, of course, in the bars of Paris (cheap and exotic drinks, pinball, space games – heaven), the Galaxian machines themselves cringe unused in the corners, rejected, gestured at. How far away their proud dawn now seems! They are leant on and eaten off, like any old Space Invader. People stub out fags on their screens. Everyone is playing PacMan, or Defending. Soon the machines will be shipped off to some seaside arcade, to wait out their days – slapped to pieces by children, their wires fizzing from the damp air, and dreaming of the great day in '79 when they invaded the space of the Space Invaders.

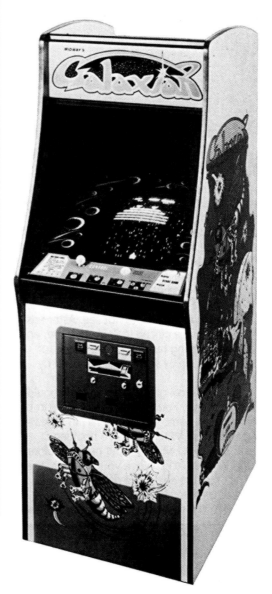

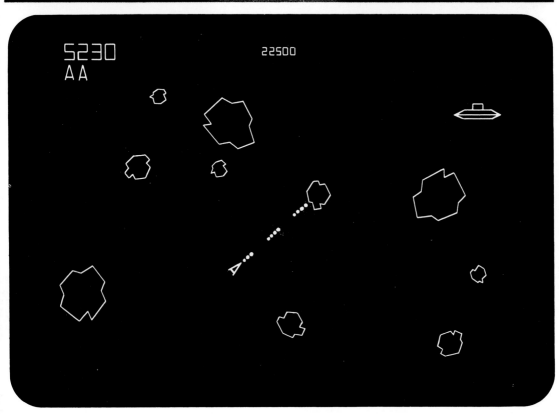

5230
A A

22500

YOU START TO CLEAR AWAY THE RUBBLE. A FATBOY CRUISES PAST.

When this book is done, I intend to start work on a cult bestseller entitled *Zen and the Art of Playing Asteroids*. Asteroids is one of the more mystical of the video games. I imagine an Asteroids tutor would resemble an old Chinese sage or guru, like the bald charlatan in the *Kung Fu* series on television. He would say that the true Asteroids player goes into a kind of trance as soon as he has put his twenty pence into the slot — a trance in which he feels and yet does not feel, sees and yet does not see. Asteroids-addicts *do* have a glazed look in their eye, and are always getting hustled by the police for dope, beaten up by skinheads, harassed by Moonies, etc.

On the charcoal-grey screen spectral boulders roll and tumble. *You* are the tiny triangle in the middle, firing bombs, or 'photons', in repeated salvoes of four. When you hit a boulder, it breaks into two; when you hit half a boulder, it breaks into two too. When you hit these, they stay hit. You fire away and dodge those asteroids until you have cleared the board.

But not so fast. Two types of saucer will assail

POINTS   20   50   100   200   1,000

you. The larger type, which we will call the Fatboy, scoots across the screen firing photons. The photons do not know where you are. The smaller type of saucer, which we will call the Pimple, scoots across the screen firing photons that *do* know where you are. They aren't random, like Fatboy's photons; they home in on you nastily. Pimple's photons, on the other hand, don't have 'wraparound'. Fatboy's photons *do* have 'wraparound'. *You* have 'wraparound': meaning that when your photons go off the board they re-enter the screen in the opposite quadrant. Hence, *lurking*.

Lurking. When the computer eggheads in California were making Asteroids (and, apparently, giving up their lunchbreaks for extra goes on their brainchild) they found that scores of 90,000 were about the best they could hope for. After 90,000, concentration slackened, the Zen trance was broken. As soon as the machine

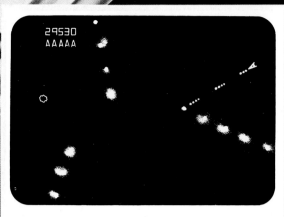

29530
ΛΛΛΛΛ

LURKING: ONE BOULDER REMAINS; SHIP LURKS
WAITING FOR INFINITE SUCCESSION OF PIMPLES.

went out on the market, however, the eggheads quickly started hearing about scores of 300,000, half a million. Where had they gone wrong?

They had underestimated the guile of the wayward geniuses who haunt the arcades. These wizards had promptly established that there was a 'safe' area on the screen. Towards the end of every wave, when only one or two quarter-asteroids remain, the machine is programmed to send Pimples at you *ad infinitum* until the last asteroids are gone. Thus the *Lurker* would lurk near the top right-hand corner of the screen and await the Pimples. If the Pimple came from the right, he would hit it direct; if it came from the left, he would get it with 'wraparound' photons. Every Pimple gave him 1,000 points. Every ten Pimples gave him a new life. Look at the illustration: each of those cones or fins at the top left-hand corner represents a life. I have seen guys with spare lives strung out three-quarters of the way across the screen – 20 lives, 30 lives! And they weren't exactly *lurking* any more either. They were swirling round the screen, blasting away with utmost confidence, on the lookout for any rash Pimples that might stray into their quadrant. Some people disapprove of *lurking*; they think it's more fun busting asteroids. I agree in a way. I would *lurk* if I could do it properly. I've tried it often. But the Pimples always seem to know where I'm *lurking*.

Asteroids machines vary more than most video games vary – not in programming but in general maintenance, in general *nick*. Some machines are wheezy old brutes, well past retirement age: scored with junk-food stains and fag burns, and all bashed about near the Hyperspace button (from panicky warp-bids, and from blows and kicks inspired by anger and exasperation), these old Asteroids are falling apart, with jammed thrust, wonky rotation, and

croaking photons. Other machines, in contrast, are smug and spruced and spanking, and wonderfully precise to the touch. Small wonder that for a long time Asteroids was the biggest money-earner in the video empire.

Asteroids is a simple game, and its pleasure could be considered monotonous by some. Coolness, dexterity and patient concentration (above all) will give you high scores and long games. But here are some general tips. **Let the asteroids come to you:** as a rule, try to stay put, near the centre of the board; any unnecessary movement increases the chances of loss of control, and in the end each asteroid is bound to pass your way. In the early stages of a wave, **break up the boulders one or two at a time:** don't go mad and reduce the whole screen to rubble – you'll find yourself dodging bricks, and will be stoned to death like an Iranian rapist. At the beginning of a wave, at least, **there is no hurry:** take your time; as long as the screen is full of boulders, Pimples are unlikely to show, and the Fatboys you can handle anyway.

This brings us to a final curiosity of the game – one I owe to an informative piece in American *Esquire*, written by somebody who clearly plays an awful lot of Asteroids. Every video game has an overload threshold, a point where the computer simply can't cope with all the elements on the screen. In Defender this

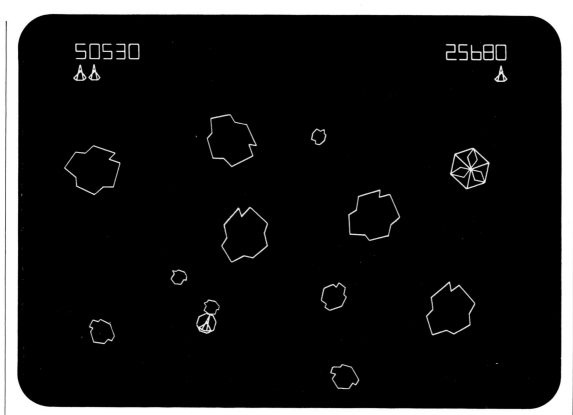

ASTEROIDS DE LUXE. RATHER MORE ACTIVE BOULDERS; SHIELD OPTION INSTEAD OF HYPERSPACE.

sometimes happens when a mass of Swarmers surges on to an already crowded screen; there is a hazy, warping effect, and some of the elements bleed to another quadrant. Sometimes, in these circumstances, you can account for a Pod with one sprayed shot: the Swarmers emerge but are crowded out by the flustered computer. In Asteroids, when the elements on screen number over thirty (boulders, a Pimple and its photons, you and your photons), the following possibility arises: if you hit a big boulder with even a single shot – it disappears! I have never done this, or seen it done, but it sounds like some good stuff to me.

ASTEROIDS DE LUXE

This is the flash variant, and one that hasn't, I suspect, been quite the hit that its manufacturers hoped for. It is basically the same game, though the boulders are projected differently and seem to roll with a stronger impression of free fall and zero gravity. The obvious innovation is the replacement of Hyperspace by the Shields option. With Hyperspace you wipe your ship off the screen, and a second later it reappears, somewhere safe or somewhere perilous; one time in three it explodes anyway, whether it collides with an

asteroid on re-entry or not. With the Shields, a little circle of light encloses and protects your ship, which gets buffeted around but doesn't break up. Shields wear out with use, and all in all they give you about the same amount of help that Hyperspace used to. But they don't, in my view, give you as much fun.

Another gimmick of the De Luxe variant is a Pod-like affair that usually comes creeping out at the end of the third wave. It looks like a tennis ball and contains three space fish, which chase you. All well and good, no doubt, all very large and fine – but the point about Asteroids was its purity, and purity is something you can't jazz up. Give me the old Asteroids every time, even the shagged-out old hulk with mangy wiring. I will show it the Way of the Dragon; I will show it, once and for all, who is the Big Boss.

KILLER SATELLITE SEQUENCE, ASTEROIDS DE LUXE.

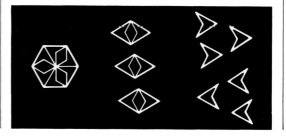

PACMAN

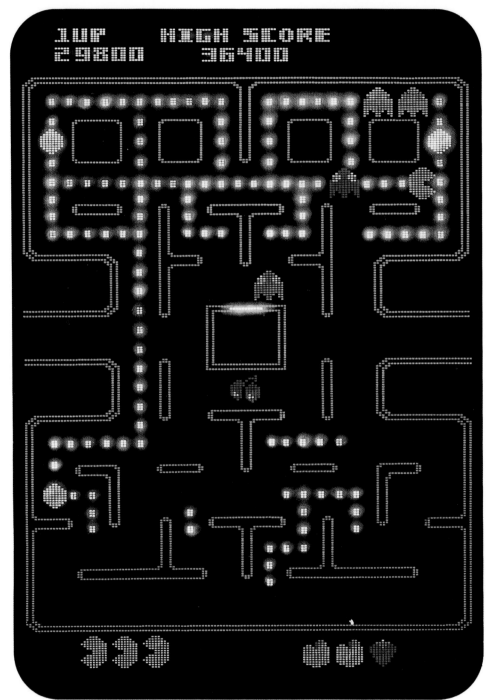

LEMON LINGERS BY A POWER-POINT, WAITING TO GOBBLE PACMEN.

PacMan is a silly idea but a good game, giving rise to an addiction that is fierce, consuming and (in my experience) short-lived. Those cute little PacMen with their special nicknames, that dinky signature tune, the dot-munching Lemon that goes whackawhackawhackawhacka: the machine has an air of childish whimsicality. It can reduce a six-foot lout – usually to be seen with a pint in one fist and a dart in the other – to helpless, giggling nursery-talk. 'Ere, look, that red bugger's munchin' after you . . . Hoo-hoo-huh-hoo! Whoops – he nearly got you

56

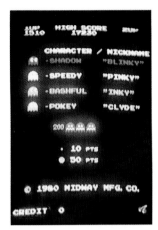

DEMONSTRATION SHEET FOR PACMAN: NOTE CUTE NICKNAMES.

then! *Cheeky.*' I once overheard two bruisers earnestly speculating about the central square (see illustration) where the enemy PacMen lurk. 'See that middle bit, where they're hiding? Go in there. See if you can go in their – in their den,' said one. '*You* go in their den,' said his friend. 'I'm not bloody going in there.'

On the other hand, I have seen bloodstains on the PacMan joystick. I have read newspaper reports of mature businessmen being dragged screaming from the console. I know a young actress with a case of PacMan Hand so severe that her index finger looked like a section of blood pudding – yet still she played, and played on through her tears of pain. I myself have spent weeks in a PacMan-fed stupor, unwilling and unable to think about anything else. PacMan sometimes seems to tower over a vast rubbish dump of rocky romances and wrecked careers. So it must have something.

What, exactly? PacMan is a grid game, a labyrinth game. Its origins are the same as those of the car games (with names like Grand Prix and Monte Carlo 2000) in which you have to dodge one, then two, then three enemy automobiles. The PacMan grid is more fluid and complicated, and there is a further refinement involving the power packs – those four flashing dots of light in the corners of the screen. The mission of the muncher, the Lemon, is to chomp its way through all the dots on the labyrinth. It is chased and ambushed by the four PacMen (**the red PacMan is programmed to follow the Lemon**; the others move randomly, with tendencies towards herd or mob groupings). When the Lemon hits the power pack, however, the roles are temporarily reversed: as long as the lights flash and the soundtrack gurgles, your Lemon can chase the fleeing PacMen, scoring 200 points for the first one it consumes, 400 for the second, 800 for the third and 1,600 for the fourth. Before you hit a power point, **linger until at least two or three PacMen are bearing down on you**. Don't forget, also, that your main business is munching dots; neglect

this fact at your peril. **And don't hoard your power packs.** I have often seen some smart-aleck greenhorn proudly surveying a board which contains four flashing power packs and hardly any dots. Boy, do they flounder! It's not only dangerous but hopelessly impractical from the PacMen-gobbling point of view. Remember that the power pack is a legitimate defensive tool – good for tight corners as well as for accumulating points. PacMan-player, be not proud, nor too *macho*, and you will prosper on the dotted screen.

Develop a system, at least for the opening gambit of each wave. On the first wave, for instance, I take my Lemon down to the bottom left-hand corner, slide it right across the base-line, weave up into the centre square, then head for one of the power packs at the top. Do I take risks in order to gobble up the fruit symbol in the middle of the screen? I do not, and neither should you. Like the fat and harmless saucer in Missile Command (q.v.), the fruit symbol is there simply to tempt you into hubristic sorties. Bag it.

Once the opening gambit has been made, you then have to play it by ear, or by eye – or, rather, by hair-trigger reflex. Go for the power packs early, as I say, and **be sparing in your use of Wraparound Avenue**. This is the lateral channel that allows you to escape from one far side of the board into the other. The Lemon goes through Wraparound Avenue at normal speed, but the PacMen are obliged to slow down. Sounds good, but you often find a PacMan waiting at the exit, and squashy disaster ensues.

And so it goes on. At 10,000 points you get another Lemon. After the second wave the machine plays its silly tune – der der derdle erdle erd der. At the bottom right-hand corner, fruit symbols are accumulated after every wave – strawberry, greengage, tomato; after a while this display runs out of room – and out of fruit: ludicrously inappropriate spaceships then appear. By this time (with the score heading towards 100,000), the Lemon is a fevered blur, hounded by a frenetic pack of PacMen. Munch your way out of *that*.

But most of us never bother. PacMania doesn't usually last that long. We're too busy doing other things – back at home nursing that splinted PacMan finger (just tell me the truth, Doctor); or on the telephone to the wife's lawyers; or joining the long queue outside the Job Centre, and generally picking up the pieces again.

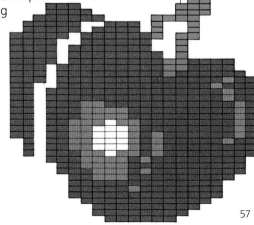

DEFENDER

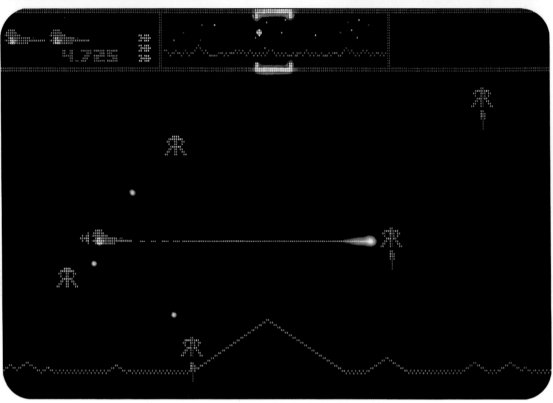

WAVE 1: EARLY TROUBLE AS THREE LANDERS PREPARE TO MUTATE.

Of all the video games Defender is perhaps the most thrilling, sinister and tortuous yet devised. It has the best colours, the best mythology, the best visuals, the best noises – the fizz of a Baiter, the humming purr of a Pod, the insect whine of the loathed Mutants as they swarm and sting. Defender is a masterpiece of the space-game challenge: real objectives, varied battle-dilemmas, gauged suspense, recurring crises – it is the ultimate test of guile, co-ordination and daring.

'You ought to be in the bleeding *Air* Force,' one young admirer said to me in a video arcade, as I swayed round a Bomber, swivelled to nail a Mutant and two Swarmers, straightened out to

nix a loaded Lander and catch his Pack, hyperspaced into centre stage before Smart-Bombing three Pods and a Baiter to clear Wave Five.

'Sure, kid,' I said, and got back to work on Wave Six. Now I do a lot of Defending. Boy, do I Defend a lot. You ought to be very grateful to me. You, or that machine, owe me *a fortune*.

Like all the best games Defender is a wallet-thinner in the early stages. If you ever see a Defender which bears the initials MLA in the All-Time Greatest column of its Hall of Fame – well, that's me, pal. I earned it. Or rather I paid for it. As the accountants at Williams Inc. know full well, **you have to spend a lot of money**

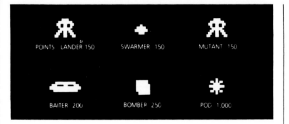

| POINTS LANDER 150 | SWARMER 150 | MUTANT 150 |
| BAITER 200 | BOMBER 250 | POD 1,000 |

to get good at Defender. That's Rule One. But the rewards are immense. Cram that dough into the slot. Listen for the machine's challenging growl.

You are travelling laterally across a spiky skyline. You are controlling your speed with the Thrust button – or the Frust button, as it seems to be pronounced in the arcades. Stars blink in the deep dark backdrop. Above the main screen is your Scanner console, which shows you the disposition of enemy forces in the entire battle area. The Scanner is a brilliant innovation: in effect, it means that you are playing on a screen nine or ten feet wide. Using the Scanner, you can police the entire battle area; you can go looking for trouble or you can, for a time, avoid it. In really fast and desperate play you look at the Scanner more than you look at the screen. Then, too, you must master the Reverse button and become ambidextrous, equally at ease whether Defending to the left or the right.

The trouble with many space games is that, once you've got the hang of them, they fail to get interesting until half-way through the battle. It is, for instance; pretty dull work dispatching the first few waves of distant, unmenacing Space Invaders. Not so with Defender, where there are long-term strategic matters to consider right from the start. The basic unit of the enemy forces is the Lander. He is your standard little-green-man, resembling a Space Invader except for his rotating eyes. He is fatal to the touch, as are all aliens, and in addition he squirts out little white bombs at unpredictable angles. Now these Landers have a mission: they are programmed to pick up the energy-packs or 'humanoids' on the skyline and carry them to the top of the screen – at which point they are transformed into the dreaded Mutants.

(A word about Mutants. Mutants are horrible creatures which look like TV-ad cartoons of the sort of germ or termite that Domestos kills. Shivering, squealing, enraged – and spitting out bombs – they home in on your ship like deadly and very experienced horseflies. 'They're bloody *vicious*, they are,' sympathized an arcade loner after I had been wiped out by the ravenous Swarm. **Always try to confront Mutants at**

the top of the screen. If you fight them on the skyline you will accidentally destroy your own Humanoids. Otherwise, **let the Mutant chase you into centre screen, then swivel and fire**.)

Prevention is the best cure, and your safest bet is to stop the Lander before he can become a Mutant. As the loaded Lander inches skywards, you must hit him cleanly, without destroying the airborne Humanoid. The Humanoid will then drop slowly, and you must catch it with the nose of your ship. This gives you 500 points; returning to the ground gives you another 500. **You can carry several Humanoids at the same time.** If the Humanoid is low down on the screen when freed from its Lander, it will fall gently back into place, awarding you 250 points. If it is higher than half-way up, it will break from the impact of its fall, and therefore needs to be safely 'fielded' by your ship. Get good at this: it is the key to successful Defending.

When and if – and heaven forbid – all ten Humanoids are ferried to the top of the screen, catastrophe strikes. The screen crackles and shudders as if in a violent electrical storm. The skyline disappears: you are in Space. All remaining Landers become Mutants. And that is normally that: you feel like a sugar lump in a beehive. Space is survivable, and some heroic, some legendary battles have been fought there. **By liberal use of your Reverse button you can sometimes divide and conquer the enemy concentrations.** But Space isn't for space cadets. **Every fifth wave your stock of energy packs is renewed to the full quota of ten**, so if you hit Space on the fourth, ninth,

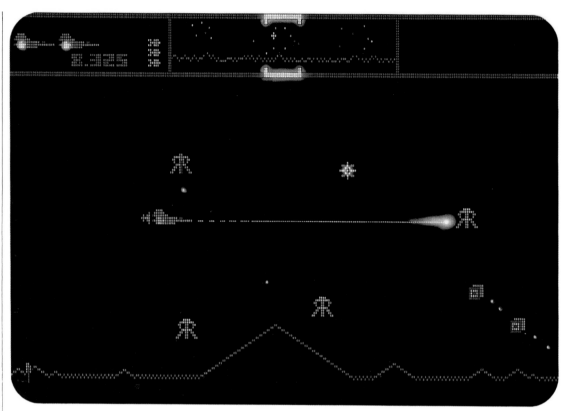

WAVE 2: BOMBERS ENTER THE PICTURE (BOTTOM RIGHT), TRAILING FATAL STARDUST; POD GLISTENS CENTRE STAGE.

fourteenth, etc., wave, you get your humanoids and skyline back once you clear the board . . . Now let's get down to some serious Defending.

THE FIRST WAVE. The First Wave is a breeze – or it is once you've invested some cash in sharpening your skills. Here you only have 15 Landers to contend with: they come surging on to the screen in three percussive salvoes. Some Landers are programmed to descend purposefully and pick up their Humanoids, while squirting out a good many white bombs (stay away from these until they are airborne); others are programmed simply to hang about the place minding their own business. If you have a lot of eager Landers in the First Wave it is possible for even an experienced Defender to get into trouble. The safest way to rescue an airborne Humanoid is to **position yourself near the top of the screen and fire in a single line:** the rising Lander will levitate into your line of fire, then you scoot forward and catch his pack. The standard score for the First Wave is 3,250 (150 × 15; plus 1,000 bonus points, 100 for each surviving Humanoid). By fielding Humanoids you can bump up your score dramatically. First-Wave scores of 13,000 are not unknown.

THE SECOND WAVE. Here we see a full cross-section of the alien forces. There is the usual squad of Landers – but also, at the outset, three Bombers and a Pod. The blue Bombers roll across the screen in wavy, lazy diagonals. They are not programmed to chase you and they do not fire bombs: but they leave a pattern of mines in their wake, which look like flecks of stardust and stay glinting on the screen for a few seconds before fading. **Get in front of Bombers,** swivel and fire. If you follow them you find yourself dodging patches of lethal stardust. Overtake, reverse, and you get a clear shot without danger.

The prettily twinkling Pods are the most benign of the alien units: they just hover and sparkle, and don't get in your hair. The trouble is that Pods contain Swarmers, and Swarmers are real little bastards. Depending on how you zap the Pod, as many as half-a-dozen red Swarmers will come whinnying out at you. **When hitting the Pod, try to fan your fire.** It is possible to catch all the Swarmers before they escape. **Don't get too close.**

Swarmers fly in loose lateral clusters, firing bombs. Once they have passed your ship they will reverse and loop back at you. This is how to nail them: let them pass, then **follow the**

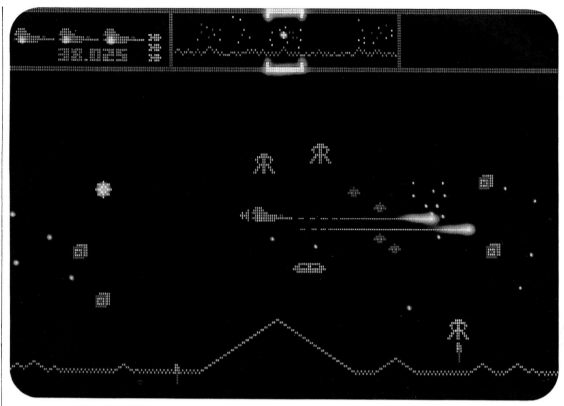

WAVE 3: FULL COMPLEMENT OF ENEMY FORCES, INCLUDING SWARMERS AND BAITERS; TIME FOR A SMART BOMB.

Swarmers at close range. They won't loop; in fact they slow down, shut up, stop firing bombs, and begin to look rather embarrassed about the whole thing.

It is likely that towards the end of the Second Wave you will have to tangle with your first Baiter. I'm sorry, but there it is. Baiters – slender, shimmying green saucers which dump bombs and home in on you without much mercy – are not part of the Wave proper. If, say, you are chasing your last Bomber to clear the Wave, and one, two, or maybe three Baiters start winging in on you – keep after that Bomber. If you get it before the Baiters get you, the Wave will end safely. Sometimes, though, a man can't run from the Baiter; sometimes a man must stay and fight. A couple of tips. If the Baiter slides off the screen, **use the Scanner to try to blast him as he slides back in.** Don't necessarily spray your shots: try firing in a continuous jet and hope he slips into it . . . But the Baiter is a bitch: emitting bombs and sharp little grunts, it hovers above or beneath you, and tries never to give you a clear shot. They're meant to send you into an end-of-Wave panic, and on the whole they do a pretty good job. Baiter time is one of the few occasions when it is worth considering the Hyperspace button on your console. 'Warp

To Another Quadrant – Caution,' say the laconic instructions by the side of the screen. The Hyperspace option is the last act of a desperate Defender. In Asteroids, the mortality rate for Hyperspace is about one in three – whether or not you warp back into a collision. In Defender, **Hyperspace gives you about a fifty-fifty chance of auto-destruction.** But when the Baiters bait like they do, when the heavens brim with bombs, and there is no escape . . . Why *not* warp to another quadrant? What the hell?

THE THIRD WAVE. I have so far refrained from any mention of the Defender's chief retaliatory weapon: the Smart Bomb. These powerful devices, which are unleashed by a deft tap of the Defender's right thumb (see illustration), instantly kill all aliens on the main screen. They are priceless offensive and strategic assets, and there are circumstances – in Space, for example – when a single Smart Bomb is worth three or four lives. In Defender you get a new life, and a new Smart Bomb, every 10,000 points. With miraculous play it is possible to hoard up a dozen lives and perhaps six or seven Smart Bombs. It is one of Defender's strengths that these bonuses are not mere extras or rewards: they are of paramount strategic importance. The

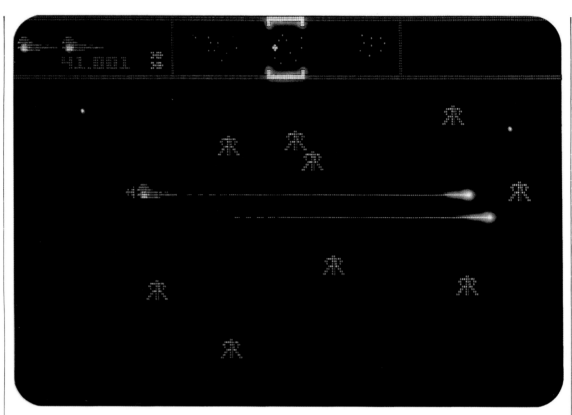

WAVE 4: PLANET EXPLODES; YOU ARE IN SPACE; ALL LANDERS BECOME MUTANTS (SEE SCANNER).

score is actually part of the game, and the shape of many a ticklish gamble is determined by whether your score is, say, 20,980 or 29,980.

I haven't mentioned the Smart Bomb earlier for a good reason: ideally, you shouldn't need to use one until Wave Three. The Smart Bomb has two primary functions: rescue from overwhelming attack (a frenzy of Mutants and Baiters, say); and the instant accumulation of large numbers of points. A well-timed Smart Bomb, with the screen crammed with aliens, can give you up to 8,000 points – which, more or less, gives you another Smart Bomb.

The Third Wave closely resembles the Second except for the fact that you have three Pods to deal with instead of one. These will appear near centre-screen at the beginning of the Wave. Now: manoeuvre so that all three Pods are on screen, then smack that Smart Bomb. With luck, you will get your three Pods (3,000 points) but **also the Swarmers inside them** (18 × 150 = 2,700). It is a wonderful moment: the screen goes muggy and soupy with a kind of nuclear aftershock; for a few seconds it is like swimming underwater.

Sometimes, you'll notice, Swarmers escape or 'bleed' into another quadrant. How to avoid this remains a vexed question which old Defenders

will discuss late into the night. There is no sure answer, but results seem to be best (a) **when Pods are widely spaced and near the edge of the screen**, and (b) **when your ship is stationary.** The Fourth and all subsequent Waves begins with *four* Pods. A successful hit will give you 7,600 points plus whatever else is in the picture. Smack that Smart Bomb, and watch your score wriggle up.

THE FOURTH WAVE. By now you will probably have lost most of your Humanoids and had quite a few Mutants to deal with. You are approaching the Fifth Wave, when your full complement of Humanoids will be restored. It is now vital that you avoid Space, with its heavy loss of life and Smart Bomb. Here it might be necessary to consider **the suicide option.** If you see from the Scanner that your last Humanoid is being carried skywards, and you know you cannot get there in time – reckon to lose a life. Just crash into the nearest alien. Then when the game resumes the Humanoid will be safely on the ground again – for a while.

Say you are down to this last Humanoid. What do you do? As the Wave begins, quickly check the Scanner for its whereabouts. (**Humanoids move**, by the way. Look closely:

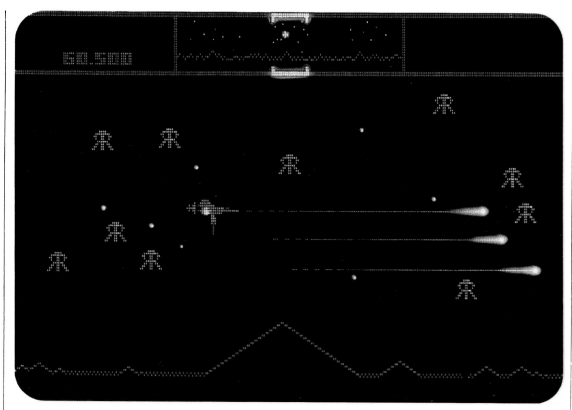

WAVE 5 AND BEYOND: SHIP CARRIES LAST HUMANOID; LANDERS MASS AND BURP OUT BOMBS HELPLESSLY. DON'T LAND THAT HUMANOID.

the packs shuffle in a sideways limp.) Go to that Humanoid and Defend it. There are two ways: you can guard the Humanoid on the ground, zapping the Landers as they queue for an opening; or else you let a Lander pick the Humanoid up, waste the Lander, catch the pack – but don't ground it! **Carry the Humanoid until you have destroyed all Landers.** The remaining Landers get a bit frantic about this ploy: look at them squirt and burp and swarm! But they are helpless so long as you keep that pack airborne. The actual shape of the terrain becomes crucial here, since you must skilfully avoid touchdown while blasting away at ground level. It is a deeply satisfying business.

THE FIFTH WAVE AND BEYOND. On the Fifth Wave your Humanoids are replenished, but things stay hot. Landers land and mutate more readily, Baiters show up sooner: a definite edge of hysteria enters the game. After Wave Five you're lucky if you have four Humanoids left; after Wave Six you're often playing guard-and-carry with your last pack. Believe me, it takes some balls to Defend your way to the haven of Wave Ten. And then it all starts again – only faster, tighter, nastier.

Before you can wipe the tears of relief from your eyes at the onset of Wave Ten – you find you're almost in Space, with all the loaded Landers shimmying skywards. Mind that Bomber! Catch that pack! Here comes a Baiter – and another! Dodge those Swarmers! Warp to another quadrant! and get a Mutant straight up your ass! The last ship explodes in silver spray. The valiant Defender lights a cigarette, marks up his score and checks to see if he has made the All-Time Greatest column, feeds in more coins, and listens to the menacing rumble as the screen *whooshes* into life. What is his dream, what is he Defending out there? He is Defending Earth, fellow Earthlings, and his own good name. He is Defending the art of Defending. He is the Defender of the Faith.

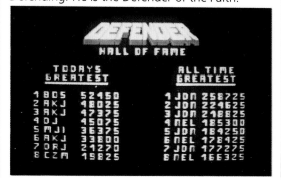

63

SCRAMBLE

DODGING SNOWBALLS WHILE BOOSTING FUEL COUNT.

This popular machine is a poor relation of Defender – a penniless nephew, in fact, furtively surviving on the family name. One of Defender's great breakthroughs was to have the space fighter travelling *sideways* into enemy territory, rather than having him simply dodge stuff

dumped on him from above. Scramble is infinitely cruder than its revered uncle, but its use of the same principle allows for a fair amount of variation and surprise.

You are travelling east over jagged and eventful terrain. Defender's three controls –

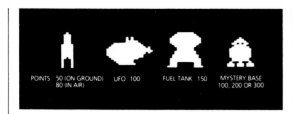

POINTS 50 (ON GROUND)   UFO 100   FUEL TANK 150   MYSTERY BASE
              80 (IN AIR)   100, 200 OR 300

altitude, thrust, reverse – are subsumed into a single, rather wiggly joystick. You have two fire buttons, Machine Gun and Bomb – lateral bullets from the ship's snout, slow-falling grenades from the belly. Beneath you on the surface are fuel tanks (which give you lots of points and boost your fuel credit) and rockets (which surge randomly upwards). The thing is to fly low, dangerously near the surface, and pick off the massed rockets and tanks.

After a while, whirly stingrays start flapping about in the air ahead of you. **Lower your speed with reverse thrust and fire in a straight line.** That should take care of these annoying creatures. Then a swarm of red snowballs comes hailing at you from the east. There is no point in firing at them; you just have to lower your speed and dodge. It's not as hard as it looks, and if you're lucky a kind of low-level Zen trance will help you out here. The red snowballs provide Scramble with its only moment of real adrenalin. After that, the terrain changes: the rockets and fuel tanks are, for some reason, perched on the ledges of a rambling skyscraper. You keep crashing into the roof of the screen. After that . . .

But why go on? Scramble is a scramble, fine as a time-waster, but quite without the logic, the coherence, the *vision* that makes good video.

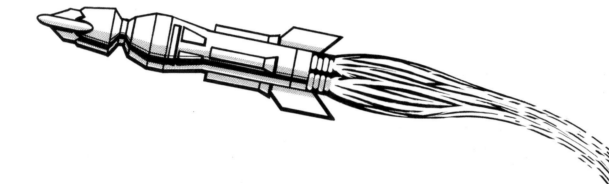

COSMIC ALIEN

Not long ago the US International Trade Commission forbade the import of 21 separate versions of Galaxian (© Bally Inc.). Cosmic Alien is presumably a domestic offshoot: it is also one of the fuzziest, furriest, shaggiest video games on the market. I first came across this garish old heap in 1979, in a kwik-food beanery on Third Avenue. It looked perfectly at home among the up-ended cartons and half-eaten blastfurters.

Cosmic Alien bears the same relation to Galaxian as tiddlywinks does to basketball. At the top of the screen there is a rack of balding budgies who, in due course, come swerving and swooping down on you. Cosmic Alien's great contribution is to have these bomb-dropping birds turn around and climb half-way up the screen again before continuing their fall. One of the mesmerizing features of real Galaxian is the way that the last two or three aliens at the end

of each wave come trickling down on you until you get them or until they get you. (I have experimented with this, by hanging around, evading but not firing, for minutes on end: they just keep coming, with the occasional sly twist or witty variation.) Cosmic Alien has a better idea: some dud genie figure appears after a few seconds to hurry you along. This guy doesn't want you sticking around having a good time. He wants you putting more money in the slot. Like all the really crappo machines Cosmic Alien is pretty difficult in its chaotic way. So high expenditure and short games can be added to its charms.

I came across another Cosmic Alien a week or two ago cowering in the middle of a rank of strapping new Gorfs and Froggers. How has this feeble wreck survived? Someone up there – a cosmic alien, maybe – must like Cosmic Alien.

LUNAR LANDER

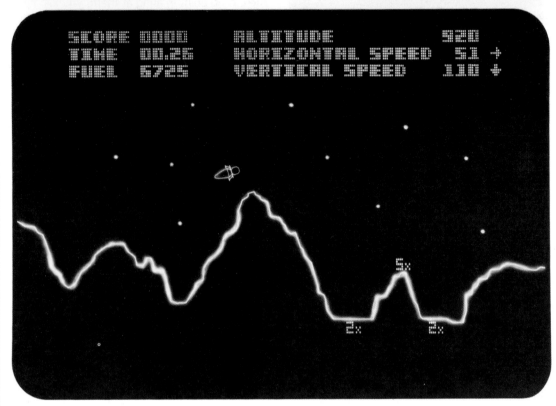

SHIP FACED WITH CHOICE OF THREE LANDING SITES.

Lunar Lander is a game for owlish adolescents and gentle old hippies. It is qualitatively different from any other game. Most video creations stress a certain sort of game-activity. Missile Command is a game of interception, Lunar Rescue of dodging, PacMan of munch-accumulation (which perhaps explains why it is the only video game with any kind of following among women). Most games, of course, are games of blasting, wasting, creaming, smashing. Lunar Lander, on the other hand, is simply a game of landing.

No ghouls or hellcats lurk on the rocky moon where Lander lands; no rockets, photons or zipships buzz its slow descent. This is a game without aliens, without adversaries. The only enemy is the player's own hamfistedness.

Like Asteroids, the Lunar screen is simply a matter of outline, white on black. The effect is well-defined, pristine, classy: it makes many of the more colourful games look like an infant's paintbox or a cutprice carpet. The Lander's module comes bleeping in over the spiky terrain. Various landing sites are indicated — graded according to difficulty (though I confess that I've never really seen the difference: once you get down to Landing, they're all pretty much the same). Rotating right or left, and steadying the pod with deft surges on the reverse-thrust console, the Lander picks his spot and gingerly

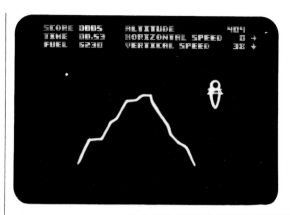 

SWITCH TO CLOSE-UP. REVERSE THRUST BRINGS SHIP IN FOR FEATHERBED LANDING.

descends, counteracting the simulated gravitational pull, friction and momentum.

As you home in on the flat landing-pad, the game pulls its best stunt: you switch to close-up. The landing then becomes a question of ticklish fine-tuning, as you adjust and correct and over-correct and re-adjust for touchdown. There are several grades of landing (good, hard, crash), as indeed there are four grades of 'mission' (Training, Cadet, Prime and Command – selectable at the beginning of the game), and points are awarded accordingly. The controls are beautifully responsive, though on any mission more advanced than Training you are going to have frequent recourse to the Abort button, which gives you escape thrust and resets the display for a fresh attempt. That little pod goes twirling out of control very easily, and no amount of thrust will tame it back into line.

The top of the screen is adorned with altimeters and speedos and fuel readings, most of which can be safely ignored. Don't bother with the readouts: just put more money in the slot.

BATTLEZONE

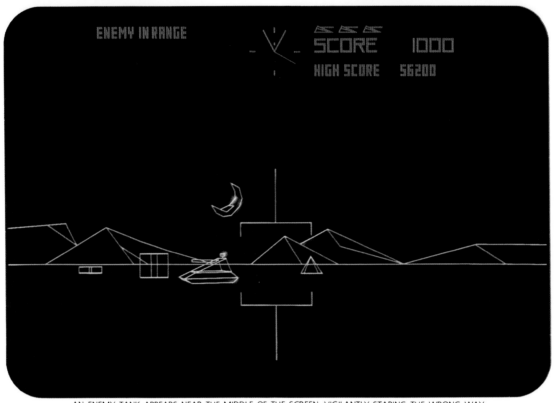

AN ENEMY TANK APPEARS NEAR THE MIDDLE OF THE SCREEN, VIGILANTLY STARING THE WRONG WAY.
BY SKILFUL NUDGES ON YOUR CONTROLS . . .

This is the futuristic tank game, with real tank controls, radar, enemy and terrain etched in diagrammatic silhouette, and wonderful accuracy of distance and perspective. This is a game of spatial awareness. It attracts a relatively middle-class and elderly audience; its patrons and admirers are intense, thin-lipped characters, whose fantasy lives are clearly of martial bent. They certainly look like officer material to me.

Admire, first, the cute controls. To begin with, I thought this was gimmickry – why not just a single joystick? But the double-fisted handlebars give a crucial sense of simultaneous forward and sideways movement, and give extra drama to the backward lurch. The radar gizmo is pretty perfunctory, but the screen is a gem, combining the look of op or pop art with the feel of a genuine battlezone: limited vision, nasty surprises, panicky adjustments while the enemy tank wheels slowly round to get you in its sights.

There are four adversaries – tank, supertank (sleeker and more mobile), Trojan Horse (swooping down from the air, vaulting obstacles, spike-nosed) and saucer (sometimes a

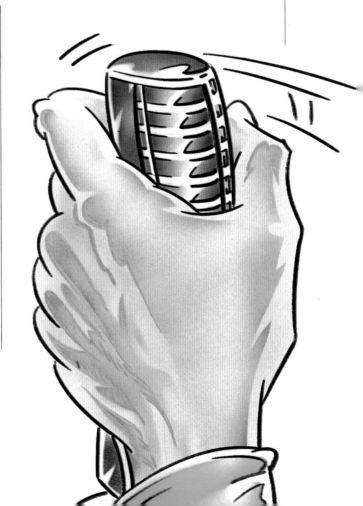

POINTS
TANK 1,000   MISSILE 2,000   SUPERTANK 3,000

BONUS TANKS
AT 15,000 AND
100,000 POINTS

SAUCER 5,000

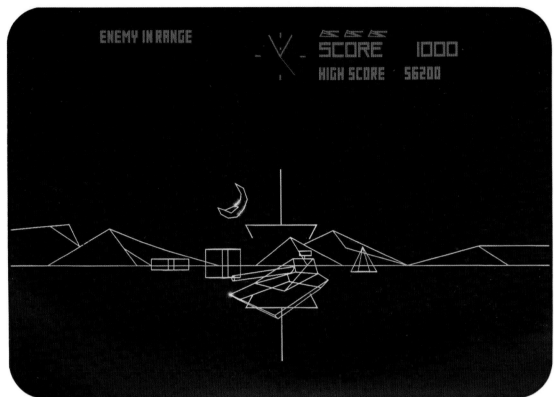

ENEMY IN RANGE

SCORE 1000
HIGH SCORE 56200

... YOU DRAW A BEAD ON THE ENEMY AS HE WHEELS ROUND TO FACE YOU. NOW YOUR
RIGHT THUMB COOLLY DESCENDS ON THE CRIMSON FIRE-BUTTON.

bleeping dot in the distance, sometimes as
colossal and immediate as the mother-ship in
Close Encounters of the Third Kind). Various
stylized transparent building-blocks provide
protection or obstruction on the bare terrain.
The radar console declares whether the enemy is
to your right or your left – or behind you. The
battle begins.

At the outset, a fat enemy tank will present
itself invitingly, quite near the centre of your
sights. You use the normal controls to draw a
bead on your foe, making the fine adjustments
by giving your handlebars gentle slaps and
shoves until you have squared yourself up dead
on line. By now the enemy tank will have sensed
your presence; it is wheeling round towards
you; you fire; the tank splinters in satisfyingly
far-flung shards. Sometimes you will seek the
protection of a building-block, and watch the
enemy tank fire furiously and uselessly at you,
seemingly only yards away. Then you reverse
and nab him when he heads for unobstructed
land.

My main piece of advice? **Go forward.** Keep

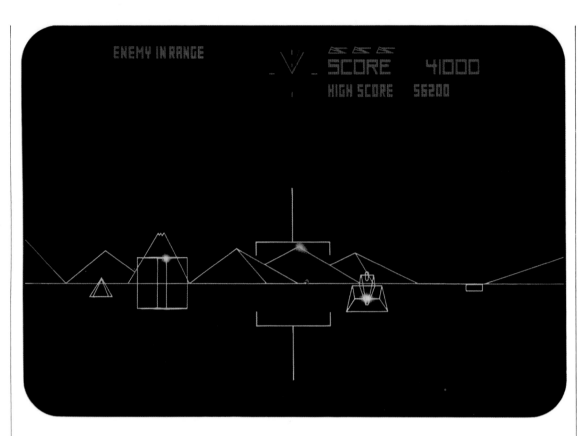

ENEMY IN RANGE   SCORE   41000
                   HIGH SCORE   56200

A SUPERTANK. THESE APPEAR MUCH LATER IN THE GAME; THEY ARE ALSO MUCH MORE AGILE THAN THEIR OVERWEIGHT COUSINS. ALREADY HE HAS YOU IN HIS SIGHTS. BRACE YOURSELF FOR IMPACT.

going forward. Sort out your first couple of tanks, then push both handlebars and go forward at top speed. Ignore the radar, which will frantically point to enemies that you are content to ignore. You'll find that nothing much happens for a while – then the big guns come at you, with their big scores. The valuable saucers don't fire at you and, furthermore, don't have to be hit dead-on. Preceded by a deep and menacing chord, the Trojan Horses jump down from the sky and career towards you: **wait until the last possible second before you hit these guys.** When your score climbs up to 20,000 or so, the supertanks start to appear. Then things get really serious.

One sees phenomenal scores in Battlezone – right up there in the six figures. These Rommels and Pattons of the arcades, they seem to know exactly what is happening, they seem to know exactly where everything is. Enemy tanks fire at them, but they have judged the angle to perfection; the shells pass them by; they retreat, they manoeuvre, they come surging in again for their hit. They dream of North Africa, of carnage at Carthage, of Thermopylae. I haven't got the stamina, or the officer qualities. I want out of this hot sweaty tank – I want to get back to base for a quiet game of Berzerk or Astro Blaster. But someone has to fight in the battlezone, and I admire these men in their vying machines.

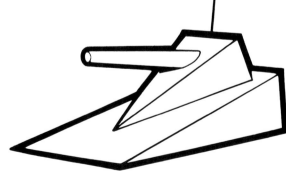

MISSILE COMMAND

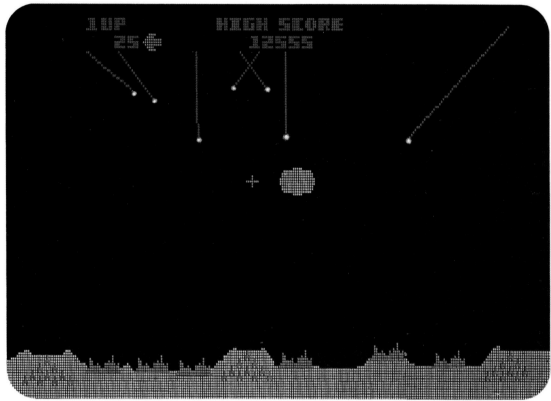

THE FUSES DESCEND; THE COMMANDER MAKES ONE INTERCEPTION AND SETS UP ANOTHER. AS YET, NO SWEAT.

Missile Command, an enigma, a mystery: one of the most beautiful and imaginative of all these curious games, and yet, and yet ... The spindly, bristling threads of the enemy fuses descend like jagged pipe-cleaners; the Missile Commander – tensed, alert, his restless legs planted well apart – rolls his magic ball. The colour of the land and skyscape in which he does battle changes gorgeously with every Wave. Like Lunar Lander, this is a gentle space game: the conflict it sets before you is one of defence and *interception*. But it is also a game in which dexterity and pure speed of reflex are more central than in any other.

And here is a confession. I just feel I ought to tell you this. Please repeat in a hoarse, hushed whisper: *'I am not very good at Missile Command.'* At 35,000 points or so, my missiles zapped, my cities in flaming tatters, the screen explodes in red and white, and the dreaded words THE END tremble before me ... There. I feel a little better now.

Some people, on the other hand, are amazingly good at Missile Command. Christ, are

they good at it. The real super-wizards tend to be Japanese, which I suppose is some comfort. When they get going, these guys are just a blur. Their decision-per-second rate would raise eyebrows at Cape Kennedy. Half bongo-player, half concert pianist, they seem to be doing about two or three dozen things at once. There is nothing for it but to stand back and watch their smoke.

That black ball on your right controls that little X, which sweeps and darts over the screen. If you press one of your three base buttons on the left, a fuse will climb upwards to meet that X, and will cause an explosion on impact with the X or with its imprint, if you have moved the ball since pressing the button. (You have a limited number of missiles per wave, and each base will beep LOW-LOW-LOW when you get down to three.)

You direct your missiles at the enemy fuses which weave and snake down on you, aiming to destroy your six cities, and coming faster every wave. On the second wave, an innocuous saucer starts gurgling across the screen. The saucer

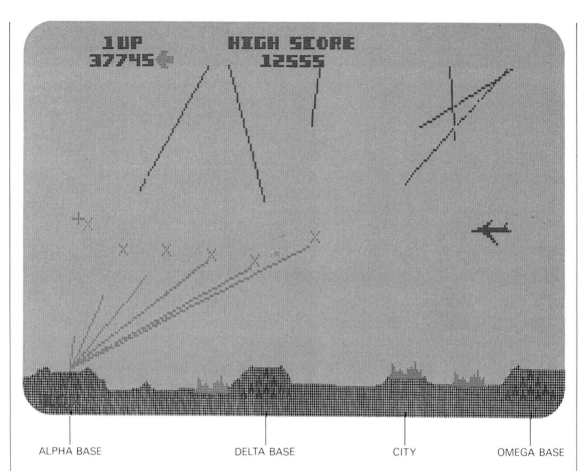

ALPHA BASE   DELTA BASE   CITY   OMEGA BASE

THE 'SPRAY' TECHNIQUE: ONE ROLL OF THE TRACK-BALL, RAPID BUTTON WORK ON ALPHA BASE.

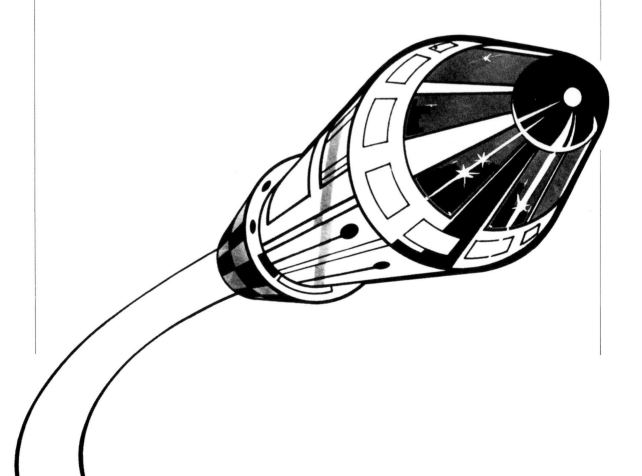

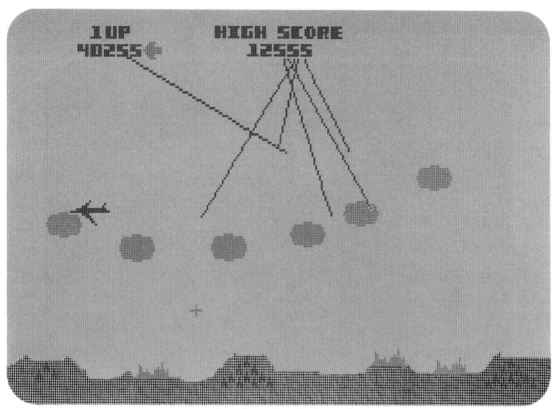

AFTERSHOCK OF THE 'SPRAY': LINKED EXPLOSIONS ACROSS CENTRE SCREEN.

doesn't drop bombs or affect the action in any way, but it is a point of pride with all Missile Commanders to nab that saucer, no matter how frenzied the battle. On the seventh wave, the diamond bombs – little silver rhomboids – begin to hail and trickle down on you. The bombs vary from machine to machine, or from logic board to logic board. Some will actually *dodge* your defensive missile explosions, climbing over the blast and continuing their fall. You just have to hit them again. Obviously the nearer these guys get to your cities, the greater the accuracy of your missiles – the greater the danger, too.

Practice and half-way normal reflexes will get you through the first few waves. Pretty soon, though, **the ambitious Missile Commander will have to master the 'spray' technique.** With one skilful, tilted swipe of the magic ball, and with six or seven rapid morse-code taps on a base button, the MC leaves a trail of X's across the screen. If the X's are well spaced, the entire middle area of the screen will be a continuous, linked explosion through which nothing can penetrate. You should be able to do this three times per wave; I always overdo it, using too many missiles in my excitement and dread. Then with your remaining missiles you pick off the diamond bombs and rogue fuses.

Clearly the successful Missile Commander must possess, or develop, the kind of spatial anticipation that I don't have – and can't seem to develop. When the first inch of the enemy fuse appears at the top of the screen, you have to know which city it is heading for. I'm forever wasting time and missiles defending cities which have already been blown to pieces. I'm forever tapping for reinforcements from exhausted missile bases. I'm forever panicking and bottling out. All I can do is watch, and wonder at, those inscrutable geniuses, way up there in Missile Command.

At 60,000 points or so the screen goes a ravishing pink. Soon afterwards it goes yellow, then white on red. At 110,000 it goes red on yellow. The task of the Commander, by this stage, is comparable to keeping a football pitch dry with a toy umbrella, during a savage downpour. But they do it somehow, until THE END.

GORF

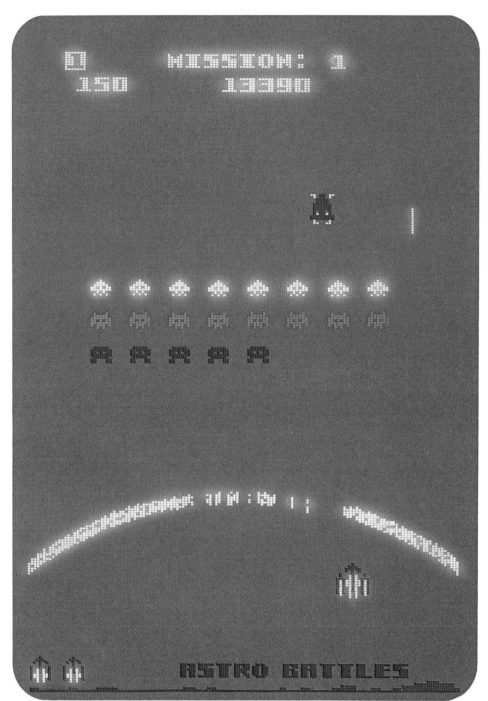

SPACE INVADER LOOKALIKES WITH CUTE GORF SYMBOL; NOTE PROTECTIVE SHIELD.

Whoever devised Gorf ought to be condemned to play the hateful thing for eternity. I fail to see why Gorf isn't at the top of every torturer's shopping-list from Ho City to Buenos Aires. After months of detailed torment – having been flogged and scourged, stomped and scorched

and peed on – the most stubborn collaborator would surely blab all after a single night with Gorf.

At first, it looks like a good idea: an anthology game. The first wave consists of a slightly jazzed-up sheet of Space Invaders, with the

"PREPARE YOURSELF FOR AN

76

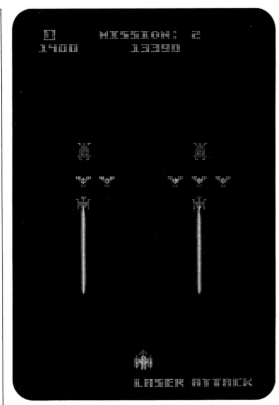

THE STAR-BURST. CIRCLING DOT HAS JUST BEEN HIT;
ANOTHER IS FORMING.

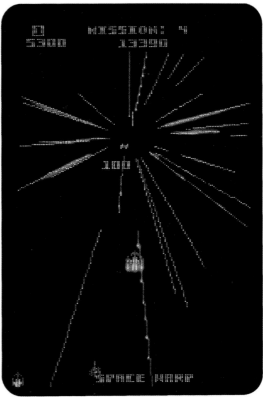

THE MOTHER SHIP. BLAST THROUGH THE INVERTED SHIELD,
SPACE CADET.

"SOME GALACTIC DEFENDER YOU ARE...."

added gimmick of a protective shield which disappears as you fire. This feels like good stuff: the player is happy with the slick new screen and with his snazzy pistol-grip joystick. Next comes a flurry of death-dealing cockatoos (which also dispense a nice vertical laser beam), followed by a round of straight Galaxians. The player's throat gets husky with nostalgia: Space Invaders, then Galaxians – just like old times.

On the subsequent wave, a tiny looping cell appears in the middle of a starburst. You have to get him while he is small and slow. Soon he starts to wheel furiously, belching out bombs. Finally a master-ship shows up, and you have to fire through your own protective shield and a mess of missiles until you nail it. Then it all starts again, faster.

Sounds fine, doesn't it? Only Gorf is a talker. Gorf talks an awful lot. Gorf taunts and goads and gloats. Boy, do you wish that Gorf would shut up. It is well known that an irritation-factor

is programmed into some machines. It makes you want to beat the machine. Well, they overdid it with Gorf. It makes you want to beat the machine *up*.

'I eat coins,' announces Gorf, with candid cynicism. He does, too: on most machines you get only two lives for your twenty pence – and then there is the more or less irresistible special offer of four lives for forty pence. Forty pence! Eight bob to be henpecked by a TV screen. Still, you pay the money simply to postpone Gorf's jeers.

'Bite the dust, Space Cadet,' scoffs Gorf. Space Cadet is the lowest and most humiliating rank. You progress through Space Captain, Space Colonel, Space General, Space Warrior and Space Avenger, depending on how many of Gorf's five-wave cycles you can dispatch. How much is it worth to Avenge yourself on Gorf? Ten pounds? Twenty? Why not keep your money, and just lob a brick through the screen?

PLEIADS

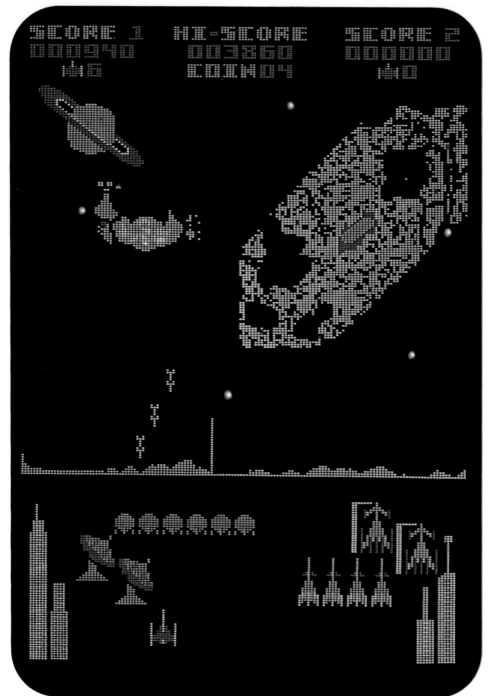

FIRST SHEET; NOTE THE OVERCROWDED SCREEN, MOST OF WHICH IS PURE DECORATION.

Launched in England during the summer of 1981, Pleiads was for a time the Great Hope of the video industry. Nowadays you only ever see the thing in kebab eateries and hamburger joints. Maybe the game is a sleeper; maybe it's a little too hectic for broad arcade appeal; or maybe no one can pronounce it. Send me a Plee-... a Pli-... a Ploi-... Forget it. Send me a Frogger.

There are four waves; or rather there are four complete changes of terrain and setting. Wave One, on this very dark and shadowy screen, has you dodging ghostly monsters and barricade-weaving insects from all kinds of unpredictable angles while you rattle out fire on your beam gun. When that's over you surge up into navy-blue space and do battle with some

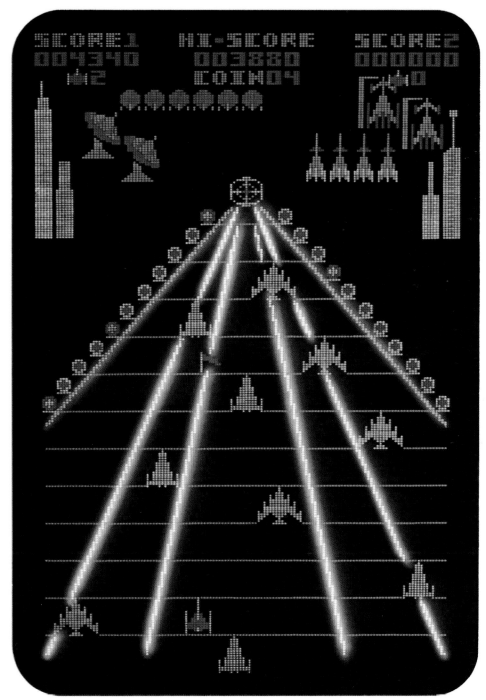

| POINTS MARTIANS NO 1 30 | MARTIANS NO 2 80 | MARTIANS UFO 150 | SPACE MONSTER: WINGS 20 CENTRE 50, 100, 400 | BONUS FLAG 100–600 | ARRIVAL TARGET 500–4,000 | BONUS: DESTROYING EACH FLEET OF MARTIANS | BATTLESHIP 0–9 600 |

LAST SHEET: NIGHT LANDING. EXTINGUISH ALL SMOKING MATERIALS.

very ordinary looping stingrays. This is random-fire stuff – a dead bore. Wave Three introduces an enemy mother-ship which has to be laboriously whacked out. Wave Four – easily the best – obliges you to return your ship to control base. It is like piloting a night landing at Heathrow or Kennedy, as you avoid the flashing obstacles on the runway. Throughout, the sound effects are good and gurgly.

The Pleiads are a cluster of small stars in the constellation Taurus. There are seven of them, though only six are visible to the naked eye. Something of the same difficulty afflicts the Pleiads' little offshoot on the video screen. Plenty going on, plenty to look at, plenty of noise: but low profile, and low definition.

FROGGER

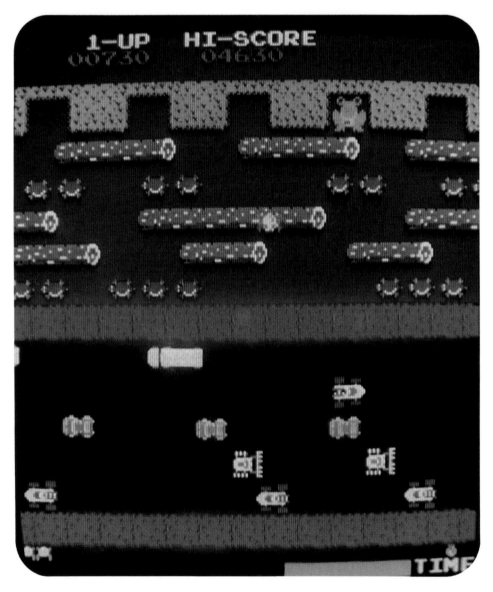

Frogger is the video industry's bid to escape from the tyranny of the space-battle motif. PacMan, with its cuteness, silly noises, and so on, pointed the way here. Both games attempt to target a lower age-group: throw down that rattle, kick out that teddybear, and reach for your piggy bank. But PacMan was a game of some complexity and sophistication, whereas Frogger, despite its early money-spinning success, just hasn't got what it takes.

You are a little green frog (can you bear this?) whose mission is to cross a busy road without being splatted, then to cross a busy river, hopping from lily to log, avoiding various turtles, snakes and crocodiles, without falling into the drink. The road is a breeze, the river a bitch. There is a quite arbitrary difficulty about getting your last frog home in the top left-hand corner. Points are accrued for each safe hop (10), for

each successful homing (50), for beating the timber (10 per second), gobbling an insect (200), squiring a lady frog to her door (200 – but what is all this?) and homing all five frogs (1,000). At 10,000 points they give you a fresh frog, but by this time you'll probably just want to throw it back.

Frogger's oldest living relative is a game called Frog. Like Frogger, Frog is capable of making you sweat with embarrassment too. Here, you have to hop up and down and catch insects of varying value with your tongue. Do we need this? You still see the odd Frog around the place, a sullen wallflower in the teeming arcades. Frog was a dog. But then, in my view, Frogger is a dogger.

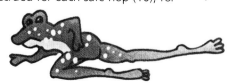

CENTIPEDE

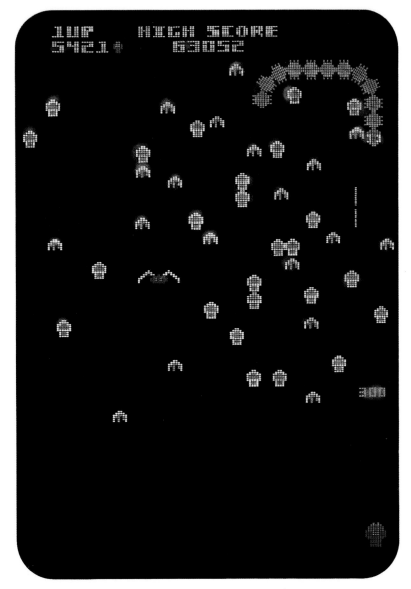

This is an insect game, coming under the sub-category of Vermin Video. I look forward to seeing new games called Dry Rot, Pest Control and Earwig. Centipede also boasts Scorpions, Spiders and Fleas. Shall I tell you how you feel after a few games of Centipede? You feel lousy.

An impressively squidgy, squiggly centipede comes wriggling down through the mushroom field towards you. If you hit him, he divides and grows a new head. Yuch! You have a fire-button and a track-ball control like the one in Missile Command, so you can venture a little way into the mushroom field if you feel like it. The centipede itself is quite easy to deal with, largely because your rate of fire increases as it gets closer, until you are almost machine-gunning the wretched creature. But other nasties lurk and swoop.

The Spider bobs around invitingly near your

turret. The Flea flits around 'laying' more mushrooms to impede your fire. The dreaded Scorpion, which carries a 1,000-point bounty on its head, moves across the board *poisoning* mushrooms. When a centipede touches a *poisoned* mushroom, it drops like a dead weight to the foot of the screen.

Centipede is a hundred laughs. Some really dedicated pesticide artists take their score right up into the six figures, and at this level Centipede seems as good a combination of skill and panic as anything to be found in the arcades. Myself, I don't much like the look of these Centurions. They have nits in their hair and straw sticking out of their ears. They scratch themselves all the time and smell strongly of ointment and carbolic. When you look at these people, you know what they mean by the phrase 'bugs in the computer'.

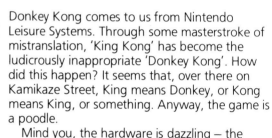

DONKEY KONG

Donkey Kong comes to us from Nintendo Leisure Systems. Through some masterstroke of mistranslation, 'King Kong' has become the ludicrously inappropriate 'Donkey Kong'. How did this happen? It seems that, over there on Kamikaze Street, King means Donkey, or Kong means King, or something. Anyway, the game is a poodle.

Mind you, the hardware is dazzling – the graphics, the sound-effects, the cartoon suppleness of the characters: all are first-rate. Kong is King of the arcades at the moment, and will probably enjoy a brief but profitable vogue. But I have a vision in which this machine is perched on top of the Empire State Building and is inexorably strafed into destruction. Donkey, your days are numbered. The knackers' yard awaits you.

The scene is an elaborate construction site. Up on top, Kong beats his chest and gloats over his capture of 'the Lady', an Olive Oyle character in a nightie. You are the Jumpman, a mild-looking hardhat in a checked shirt. 'Jump button makes Jumpman jump' – as if you hadn't guessed. When the Jumpman has a hammer in his hand, he is invincible. Jumpman has to scale the ladders and ramps, jumping over the barrels and other missiles which Kong unleashes on him. When he reaches the top, the Lady looks pleased, Kong goes ape-shit, and a pink heart blooms briefly at the top of the screen. Then Kong picks up the chick and heads off to the second wave. Now the site gets even more elaborate, with pulleys and lifts and whatnot. If Jumpman gets to the top a certain number of times, Jumpman saves the Lady. You have to be over eighteen to see what he does to her next. Then it all starts again.

Enough? It is more fun to speculate what Nintendo will bring us in the future. The Missing Lynx. The Loch Ness Marmoset. The Puppy from 20,000 Leagues.

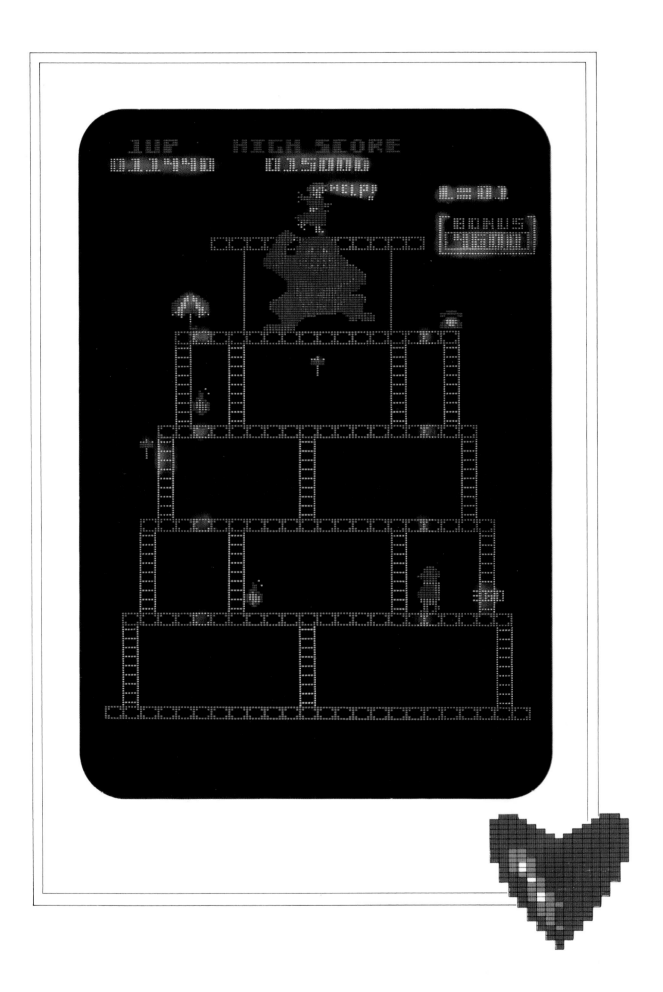

TURBO

Turbo is the very latest from Gremlin Industries. It has not yet reached British shores (though apparently a couple of them have landed and are in hiding down at Eastbourne), so I can give you only a few impressions of the game, gathered from advance publicity and from the hushed, cancel-eyed gossip of the arcade space-wanderers.

Racetrack games have been growing in sophistication for the last ten years or more. Such was the authenticity on display that one expected to emerge from the cockpit covered in

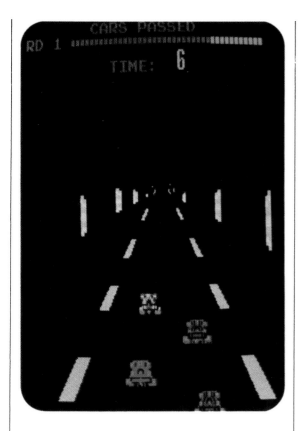

grease. There were flags, headlights, bone-crunching crashes. But Turbo looks as though it breaks new ground – video ground, too. Some race games are (so to speak) the pits; Turbo, clearly, is the tops.

For a start you get your simulated cockpit driving-seat, pro-rally steering wheel, 2-speed shift, and flickering dials. What else is new? You're not on a racetrack: it's more like doing your driving test at a hundred miles an hour. Snow, roadhogs, veering ambulances, traffic,

tunnels, blind bridges – all in terrain changing from alpine to Manhattanesque.

It sounds rather like *driving*, doesn't it? Later models will probably provide you with a window to wind down and shout out of. Soon it will be impossible to enter a video arcade without getting run over. Gremlin will decide to save a bit of money, and put the punters in cars instead.

These are the games for the armchair sportsman. They have one rather serious flaw. Playing Video Hustler, Pro-Golf and Dribbling does not approximate to playing pool, golf and football. It approximates to watching pool, golf and football *on television*. You are not at one remove from the real thing. You are at two removes. And two removes is one remove too many.

VIDEO HUSTLER is the pool game (courtesy of Paul Newman). The balls jink and roll about quite convincingly, and the pockets gape as wide as they do on the real thing. The problem is: how to aim? You control the direction of the cue ball by positioning a marker on the edge of the table. The cue ball will head for that marker, the force of the shot being determined by three selectable levels. It's difficult enough lining up a tricky pool shot, judging weight and angle and so on. Imagine trying to do this *from above*, with only a target on the far cushion to aim at. Very difficult, no? Pool is all about eye-line. In comparison, Video Hustler is like playing marbles.

PRO-GOLF combines two great Japanese obsessions: golf and video. The screen is in two sections, the lower half showing the immediate action on the ball, the upper section showing the complete course for each hole (along the lines of the Scanner unit in Defender). To the strains of an irritating ditty, a smartly dressed young lady marches up to the tee. You choose her club with a lever, and also determine the flight of the ball. She 'addresses' the tee and takes five swings, the last of which is automatic if you have failed to punch your red button. There are trees, ponds and bunkers, birdies, pars and holes-in-one (which score 30,000 points). When you run out of balls, which in my experience happens after only a few seconds, the machine will incite you to put more money in before time runs out. There are nine holes: this is an improvement on eighteen. The only place to play this game, however, is in the 'nineteenth hole', with a big drink and lots of friends to restrain you from setting about the screen with your heaviest iron.

DRIBBLING is the football game. A lot of time, money and ingenuity has been expended here, only to convince you that the old bar-football is infinitely superior. For one thing, bar-football actually has a *ball* – what a gimmick! It doesn't seem to have occurred to the video eggheads that football has a much greater natural affinity with a mechanical game than with an electronic one. We are left with an image of the ultimate folly of the video age: a man walking past a pool table for a game of Video Hustler instead. It *must* be better: it's on television, isn't it?

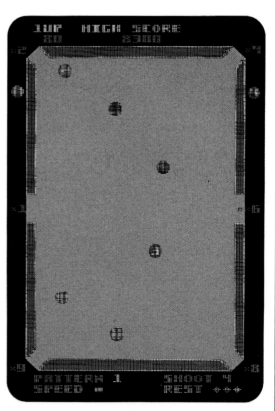

DRIBBLING

VIDEO HUSTLER

PRO-GOLF

TEMPEST

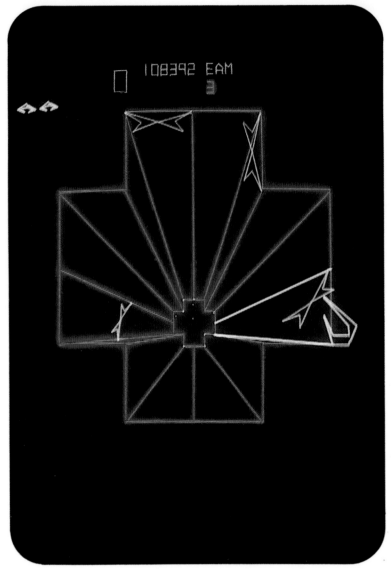

SKILL-LEVEL 3 (SEE DIGIT). FLIPPERS TWANG AROUND THE RIM OF THE STAR-GATE.

Tempest burst on to our screens just as this book was going to press. Despite long vigils in the arcades, I had some trouble getting a go on this compelling creation. As is always the case in arcade-land, a new machine causes a good deal of communal excitement: kids are draped all over the console, and long queues form, edging slowly towards the altar of the screen. I had plenty of time to study the logo-graphics of the hardware: depicted on the unit's crest was the usual snarling monster. But once I got up front – whew! – and bagged my turn, I quickly saw that Tempest was the least monstrous and most abstract game yet devised. It is, in short, a breakthrough.

'You' are a claw-like, bomb-dispensing gizmo which hops and hurdles over the rungs of a geometrical figure, made up of a dozen-or-so channels along which multi-coloured enemies stream continuously outward. The waves are short and the geometrical figure changes dramatically and often. At one point you are on the tip of a cone, and seem to be staring down into abysmal depths where the enemies mass and gurgle; at another, you are at the receiving end of an infinite spectral bowling-alley, with the enemies teeming down the lanes towards you. The brilliantly flattened and extended perspectives are an obvious tribute to the 'stargate' passage in Kubrik's *2001*. There is

OPPOSITE: TWIRLY GREEN SPIKERS, SQUARE FLIPPER TANKERS (CONTAINING FLIPPERS) BOMBS
DESCENDING FROM DEFENDING CLAW, (OR BLASTER).

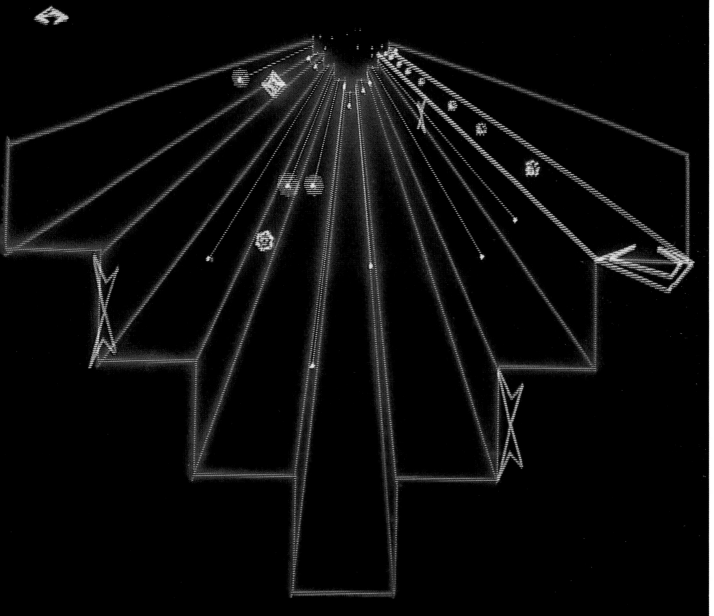

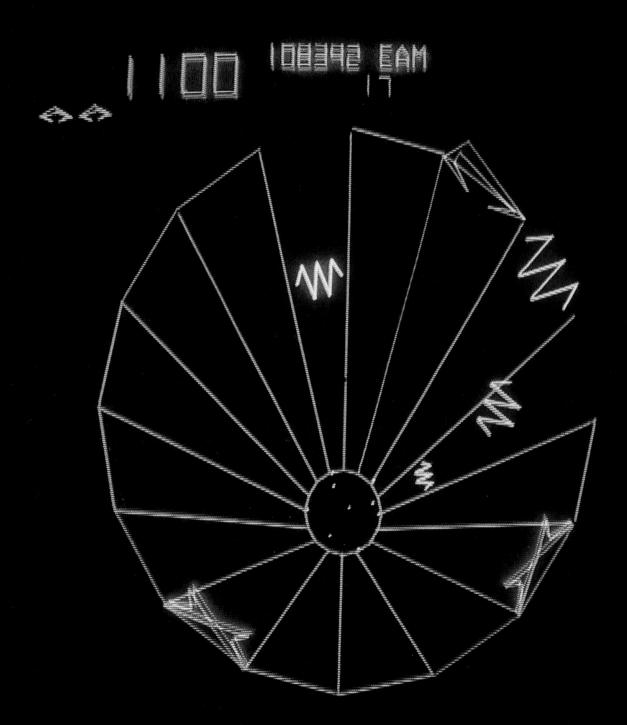

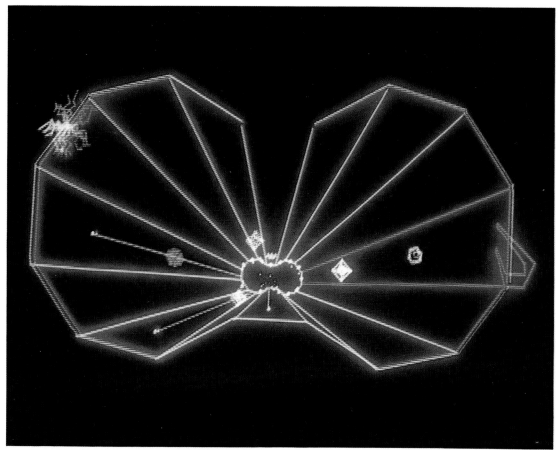

FUSEBALLS: LEVEL 11. FUSEBALL-TANKERS AT LEVEL 33.

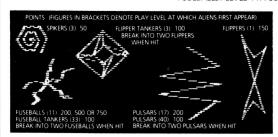

POINTS (FIGURES IN BRACKETS DENOTE PLAY LEVEL AT WHICH ALIENS FIRST APPEAR)

SPIKERS (3) 50   FLIPPER TANKERS (3) 100   FLIPPERS (1) 150
                  BREAK INTO TWO FLIPPERS
                  WHEN HIT

FUSEBALLS (11) 200, 500 OR 750   PULSARS (17) 200
FUSEBALL TANKERS (33) 100   PULSARS (40) 100
BREAK INTO TWO FUSEBALLS WHEN HIT   BREAK INTO TWO PULSARS WHEN HIT

something genuinely other-worldly about this machine; here, you tangle with alien latitudes.

There is no messing about with shot-rapidity: you keep your finger on the Fire button continuously. You have a Superzapper button which is the equivalent of a Smart Bomb, killing everything on the screen. At the end of every wave you go through a Superzapper Recharger. This device, unsurprisingly enough, recharges your Superzapper. (It is a minor defect of the machine that you cannot save up your Superzappers for the more difficult waves: one per sheet, and that's your lot.) Meanwhile the enemies flow outward. They look like crystals or like polychrome American cereal – here they come, zap, crackle and pow. Some are far more dangerous than others. The purple hot-cross bun, for instance, divides into two grappling-hooks when hit; if the hooks reach the end of the lanes, they swing about with lethal speed and are very hard to nail. Reach for your Superzapper, if you still have one. I have yet to familiarize myself fully with the enemy arsenal. The laconic instructions on the console are particularly unhelpful in this respect: 'Kill pulsar by: Shooting at it when it is not pulsing.' Yes, but which is the pulsar?

There are further gimmicks and attractions. There are ten skill-speed levels, and you make your selection before commencing battle. At the end of the game you are given your position out of the top 99 scores. (Plenty of scope for humiliation here: I never got beyond 37th.) After a couple of waves a new hazard looms. You are contentedly waiting for your Superzapper to be Recharged when suddenly the following words flash on to the screen: AVOID SPIKES. Before you know it, you have been skewered by a green laser. Be vigilant for this, and look for the safe channels before the words appear. After a while, they don't even warn you.

Welcome, O Tempest. You will last far longer than all the new machines with names like Daddy Longlegs and Pro-Celebrity Tiddlywinks. You and I have a rendezvous. I will see you around.

OPPOSITE: PULSARS: THEY APPEAR AT LEVEL 17 AND ARE VERY DANGEROUS. AT LEVEL 40, PULSAR-TANKERS SHOW UP: THEY BREAK INTO *TWO* PULSARS WHEN HIT.

PART 3

FIGHTING BACK FOR MOTHER EARTH:
BEATING THE GAMES

INVASION OF PRIVACY

Domestic video has been around the house for nearly ten years now. TV-attachment games are nothing new: they have simply been thrown into exorbitant prominence by the arcade boom. Naturally, as the boom shows signs of falling off, the electronic nabobs are looking hungrily to the home market as the true mother-lode of the video-game industry.

They will be proved right. It has to happen. The shape of modern life has established television as 'the medium', in Gore Vidal's phrase. From the historic day when Nolan Bushnell started tampering with the family set, the destinies of television and the Space Invader have been inextricably entwined. It is all of a piece, is it not? In a decade or two there'll be no good reason for stepping out of the front door: you can just loll about the house, feasting your senses on a never-ending serial of Electric Blue,

The Sting and Asteroids de Luxe. By then, people will have take-away pizza parlours in their own homes.

'These are not toys; this is family entertainment,' says an Atari consumer-division high-up. 'Eventually people will want them like they wanted a television set.' In the 'fifties, first-generation TV-owners found themselves curiously effected by this flashing eye in their living-rooms; many people were so convinced that they were 'being watched' that they were reluctant to undress in front of the screen. What effect will the Space Invaders have? I predict a boom in the 'eighties for sandbags, gasmasks, radiation shelters.

No matter. Before long the green monsters will have forced their way into every self-respectingly affluent home. The Invasion will then be complete.

TV GAMES: THE RUN OF THE CARTS

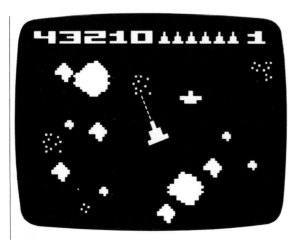

ASTEROIDS (ATARI)

So how do we start? First, you go out and buy your Atari or Videopac or Activision or Intellivision or Compellivision or Hellivision unit. Inflation makes them seem quite cheap. Then you frown at the instruction booklet: here is your co-axial cable, your aerial switch box, your game power cord. The next task is to take the game power cord and put a plug on it. I may be unrepresentative here, I realize, but this challenge cost me 45 minutes, three fingernails, two cigarettes, and a whole thesaurus of obscenities. Now you *plug in* the game power cord, monkey with the aerial switch box, and 'tune' your television to an unused channel. Abracadabra! The word Pellmellivision, or whatever, appears on the screen! Let the game begin!

First, a warning – before the eyes mist over, the lower lip starts to tremble, and the whole venture collapses in hot tears of disappointment. *Home video is not the same thing as arcade video*. To begin with, as you sit with your formica console on your lap, twiddling your toggle stick, you think: 'They're *kidding*.' One had heard that the TV version lacked some of the precision of the parlour mastersets – but even so. This, however, is precisely the association one has to suppress. The two things are chalk and cheese.

In terms of sophistication, the home games are several years behind their big brothers on the shop floor. Appropriately enough, they are about on a level with Television Breakout. Take Space Invaders itself. I have been Invaded by several of the TV versions. In one game, it is more or less impossible to control your defending turret; you can't even keep the thing still. In another, the disintegration of your home barricades has been reduced to mere stylization: every time it receives an alien bomb, an exact quarter of the barricade simply disappears. For someone who has never played the real thing – and I suppose such people still exist: in unexplored corners of Siberia, maybe – the TV version is a perfectly adequate game. For the jaded lounge-lizards of the arcades, on the other hand . . .

Soon I was frisbeeing the cartridges – or 'carts', as they're called – all over the room; they were being hurled over my shoulder like chicken-legs at an Elizabethan banquet. Tank Pong, Armor Battle, Laser Blast, Astro Smash . . . The typical combat game presents you with a one-against-one set-up of variable ingenuity; it is always better to play these games with a friend rather than against the machine, since you can then share the disadvantage of limited mobility. Some games are obvious turkeys – real back-to-the-drawingboard stuff. In Shooting Gallery, the field is so crowded that you are

SPACE INVADERS (INTELLIVISION)

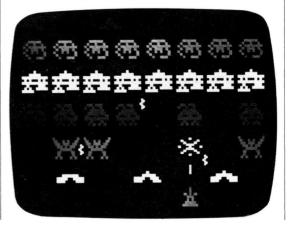

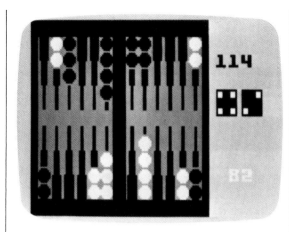

BACKGAMMON (INTELLIVISION)

more or less reduced to random fire; and the fastest-moving targets move faster than your bullets, so only a fluke shot can nail them.

By far the best carts – for anyone over the age of ten – are simply televisual versions of normal domestic games. Draughts faces you with an almost unbeatable opponent. Backgammon faces you with a stolid percentage player. As is the case with computer chess, the machine is programmed with only the more obvious directives. It likes taking your men off so much that it is pretty well helpless in the face of a shrewdly timed backgame. It likes making bays so much that its defences tend to be unprofitably spaced out: you seldom have to tackle anything remotely approaching a sideprime. The machine, of course, doesn't double – but it doesn't seem to cheat either. All the dice-rolling takes place on screen (accompanied by a not particularly irritating jingle) and one is inclined to murmur skeptically

CHESS (INTELLIVISION)

when Atari, or whichever, rolls the occasional double six. The machine loses with good grace and is always amenable if you want another game. Naturally, the gambling element is missed here – and missed sorely, missed achingly, in Blackjack and Poker. In normal poker, the presence of money is not just a frill: bets are no less important than the cards themselves. Ace, King, Queen, Jack means nothing without money to say, or to see, whether there is a Ten in the hole.

The sport games – Boxing, Skiing, Tennis, Horse Racing, Basketball, Fishing Derby (what next? Hang-gliding? Windsurfing?) – can be fairly challenging in their limited-option way. Tennis, for instance, with its choice of shots and positions, has certainly come a long way from Nolan Bushnell's tremulous dream. And a lot of imagination, not all of it whimsical, has gone into background noises and effects.

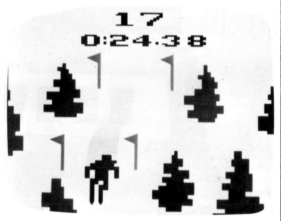

SKIING (ACTIVISION)

Meanwhile, one simply hangs around waiting for the games to get better. Once, in a futuristic treetop house in Palm Beach, Miami, I played home-video Space Invaders on a screen ten feet wide, at double speed, with wiggly bombs, no barricades, invisible invaders – all the gimmicks. Back in the street-corner coffee shop, I lazily slid a quarter into the old Taito prototype. It was still the better game, no question. But already I have seen TV Invaders in video showrooms that do quite a passable imitation of the real thing. Unquestionably the day will come when we can sit propped up by pillows and capably defend Earth on a screen at the end of the bed. By that time, the machine will probably be able to wake you up, make you coffee, answer your letters, do your work, cook you lunch and turn you over for a good night's sleep. The day will come. But it hasn't come yet.

ACETRONIC MPU 1000/2000 (similar to the Interton VC-4000, Radofin 1292/1392, Prinztronic VC-6000, Teleng, Rowtron and Database computer-game systems).
Features: 2 hand sets with multi-directional joysticks, sound effects, colour and automatic on-screen scoring.
Cartridges available: Air/Sea Battle, Basic Maths, Black Jack, Breakout, Challenge, Chess, Code Breaker, Draughts, Golf, Grand Prix, Horse Racing, Invaders, Maths 2, Musical Games, Othello, Pinball, Polympics, Prize Fighter, Shooting Gallery, Soccer, Super Maze, Tank/Plane Battle and Treasure Hunt.

PHILIPS VIDEOPAC G7000/MAGNAVOX ODYSSEY²
Features: alpha-numeric keyboard, 2 hand sets with multi-directional joysticks, sound effects and colour.
Cartridges available: A Pac (everything you need to know to put your own message on the screen), American Football, Baseball, Basketball, Basket Game, Battlefield, Billiards, Catch the Ball/Noughts and Crosses, Chinese Logic, Cosmic Conflict, Dam Buster, Flipper Game, Football, Golf, Gunfighter, Introduction to Computer Programming, Jumping Acrobats, Laser War, Marksman/Depth Charge, Mathematician/Echo, Monster from Outer Space, One-armed Bandit, Pairs/Logic/Space Rendezvous, Pharaoh's Secret, Playschool Maths, Quest for the Rings, Race/Spinout/Cryptogram, Samurai, Satellite Attack, Slalom, Stone Sling, Supermind, Take the Money and Run, Tanks/War-planes/Submarines, Team Sports, Ten-pin Bowling, The Musician and Volleyball.

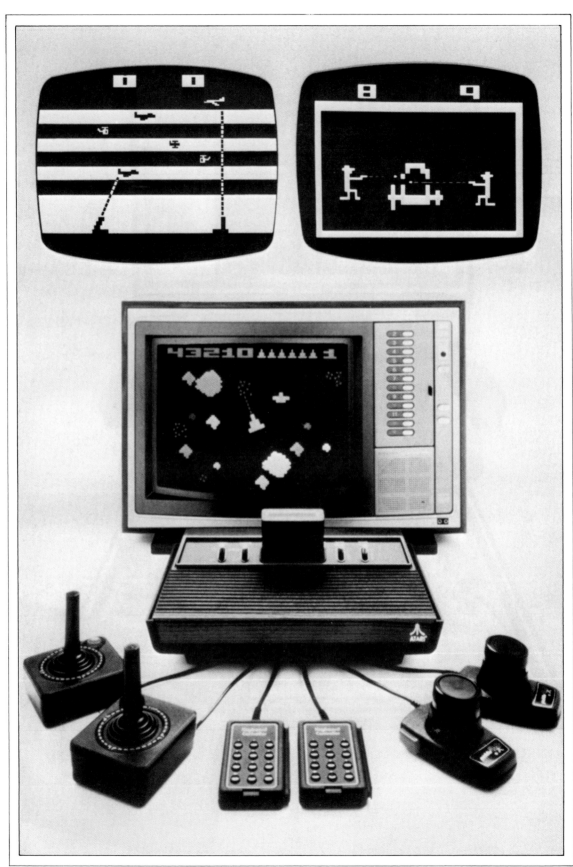

ATARI VIDEO COMPUTER SYSTEM

Features: 2 hand sets with multi-directional joysticks with command button, 2 paddle controls with command button, colour, sound effects and automatic on-screen scoring.

Cartridges available: Adventure, Air-Sea Battle, Asteroids, Backgammon, Basic Maths, Basic Programming, Basketball, Bowling, Brain Games, Breakout, Casino, Championship Soccer, Circus Atari, Codebreaker, Combat, Concentration, Dodge-Em, Golf, Hangman, Human Cannonball, Indy 500, Maze Craze, Miniature Golf, Missile Command, Night Driver, Outlaw, Skydiver, Slot Racer, Space Invaders, Space War, Street Racer, Superman, Surround, Video Checkers, Video Chess, Video Olympics and Video Pinball.

Activision cartridges available for use with the Atari Video Computer System: Boxing, Dragster, Fish Derby, Freeway, Karboom, Laser Blast, Skiing, Tennis, Chicken Crossing the Freeway, Barnstorm, Grand Prix and Stampede.

INTELLIVISION

Features: 2 hand controllers, 12-button touch-sensitive numerical key pad with 4 action keys, 16-directional object movement disk, sound generator capable of producing 3-part harmony, colour, in-built mains transformer. Add-on keyboard for conversion into home computer in production.
Cartridges available: Armour Battle, Astrosmash, Auto Racing, Backgammon/Poker/
Blackjack, Basketball, Bowling, Boxing, Checkers, Dungeons and Dragons, Football, Golf, Hockey, Horse Racing, Maths Fun, Roulette, Sea Battle, Skiing, Snafu, Soccer, Space Armada, Space Battle, Tennis, Triple Action, Word Fun.

AMONG
THE ALIEN CORN

The first wave of handheld toys appeared during the festive season of 1980. I remember watching a tubby 10-year-old saunter down a London street while simultaneously zapping a fistful of Space Invaders. He was using a Galaxy Invader, courtesy of Computer Games Ltd. Galaxy Invader is the size of a small dustpan, featuring three channels down which the invaders bob and flash, dodging the shots from your manoeuvrable missile station. With enemy master ship and three skill levels, this was not a bad little game.

Galaxy Invader 1000 is the same game with a few cosmetic extras. Jet Fighters is the same game too, transferred to a naval setting. Various additional offshoots kept to a similar format: Earth Invaders, a maze game; Gun Fighters, the arcade Boot Hill; Grand Prix, a car-racing game – and so on.

Then a new generation of games was born: not handheld so much as coffee-table in their dimensions. Space Invader, Astro Invader, Galaxian, Super Space Invader 2, and whatnot. Like Galaxy Invader, Space Invader and Super Space Invader 2 travesty the arcade Space Invaders. Like Astro Invader, Galaxian travesties – hold your hats – the arcade Galaxian.

Of these second-generation toys, one looks more promising than the rest, because the arcade game it exploits is reduceable to the small scale. I refer to the PacMan spin-offs. Even

here, though, you must tread carefully. Packri Monster, for instance (The Challenge! Gobble or Be Gobbled!), is an abject little unit. My model broke down after precisely one game, and is now capable only of the occasional neurotic tweet and gibber. PacMan 2, on the other hand, from Entex Inc., is a winner – the first handheld game of any merit at all. The controls are

clumsy, the enemy PacMen are rather too unpredictable in their movements, the gobble-time lasts too long: but here is a game that generates its own special excitements. It is even mildly addictive, God bless it.

For a month now I have been test-driving these new toys. I have to stay in all the time because more deliveries are always on the way.

My small flat is infested with plastic and styrofoam. They lurk in the laundry basket, under the bed, behind the typewriter. I tried to dry my hair with one the other day. Another I mistook for a toaster, and tried to cram some bread into it. I stub my cigarettes out in them. I once took a bite out of Earth Invaders, thinking it was a Big Mac. I know it's all popcorn anyway.

The range of handheld video games is enormous. Here are some examples of the many different types on the market.

EARTH INVADERS (CGL)
Game: player-controlled soldier (red) digs holes and tries to bury invaders (green) that fall into them before being destroyed by other invaders. Failure to bury the invader properly results in it re-emerging. Spec: two skill-levels. Three ascending levels of play. Maximum point score: 9,999. Maximum time limit: 13 minutes. Optional mains transformer.

MICROVISION (MILTON BRADLEY)
Games: Blockbuster (knock out blocks in a three-layer wall); Bowling; Shooting Star (aerial target-shooting); Pinball; Connect Four (strategy game); Sea Battle; Space Vaders. Spec: liquid crystal display. Handheld console supplied complete with Blockbuster cartridge. Other cartridges purchased when required.

PACKRI MONSTER (BANDAI)
Game: PacMan variant. Spec: multi-coloured fluorescent screen. Joystick control. AC adaptor available.

SPACE INVADER (ENTEX)
Game: Space Invaders. Spec: multi-shaped brilliant LED vessels. Two skill-levels. Progressive degrees of difficulty.

PACMAN (ENTEX)
Game: PacMan must attain as high a score as possible by capturing ghosts, bugs and energizers without being himself destroyed by the ghosts. For one or two players. Spec: multi-coloured fluorescent display. Six skill-levels. Difficulty varied by both selection of skill-level and quantity of ghosts programmed in the one-player game. Silent or sound option. Built-in AC adaptor jack.

GUNFIGHTERS (CGL)
Game: gun-slinging. Player v. computer-controlled gunfighter opponent or two players v. each other. Spec: liquid crystal display. Choice of skill-levels and stance of gunfighter (standing, prone and crouching). Random obstructions and comprehensive sound effects.

RAISE THE DEVIL (ENTEX)
Game: pinball. Spec: LED indicators. Four skill- and six speed-levels. Full pinball functions, including bumpers, flippers, flashing lights, sound effects, etc. Auto score-keeping.

ASTRO INVADER (ENTEX)
Game: version of Space Invaders. One or two players. Spec: three-colour fluorescent display. Two skill-levels. Silent mode option. Increasing degrees of difficulty. AC adaptor jack available.

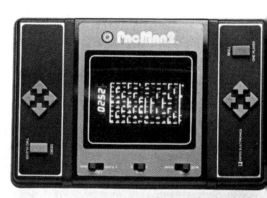

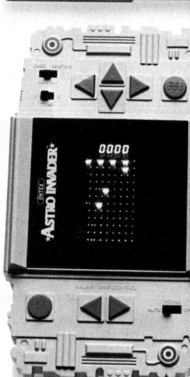

ALAXIAN (BANDAI)
ame: Space Invaders. Spec: super-bright, multi-colour fluorescent read-out. Four rows of
vaders. Two skill-levels. Varying angles of attack from aliens. AC adaptor available.

ALAXY INVADERS 1000 (CGL)
ame: Space Invaders. Spec: two-colour fluorescent display. Three skill-levels. Three rows
invaders and three missile launch positions. Sound generator. Optional mains
ansformer.

TFIGHTERS (CGL)
ame: air/sea battle. Player defends missile base against rocket-firing jetfighters launched
om enemy battleships. Spec: two-colour fluorescent display. Three skill-levels. Maximum
int score: 199. Sound generator. Optional mains transformer.

MOLE PATROL (BANDAI)
Game: players score when farmer strikes mole with hammer. At the same time the player
protects the farmer from other moles which appear from below and try to bite the
farmer's foot. Injured farmer is taken to hospital by ambulance and the game ends when
all the hospital beds are filled. Spec: multi-coloured fluorescent display. Four skill-levels.
Comprehensive sound effects. Fast arcade action. AC adaptor available.

SUPER SPACE INVADERS (ENTEX)
Game: Space Invaders variant. Spec: two-colour fluorescent display. Three skill-levels. Silent
or sound option. Maximum point score: 999. Built-in AC adaptor jack.

GRAND PRIX (CGL)
Game: motor racing. Spec: LED display reproducing sections of a racetrack circuit.
Player-controlled car can be accelerated, braked and steered from lane to lane by two
mini-joystick controls to avoid computer-controlled opponents.

LED = light-emitting diode

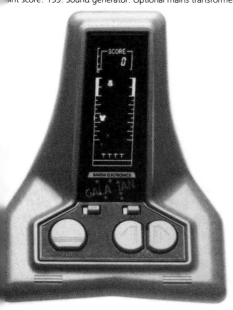

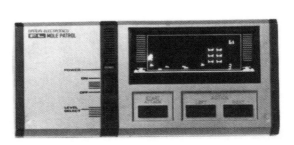

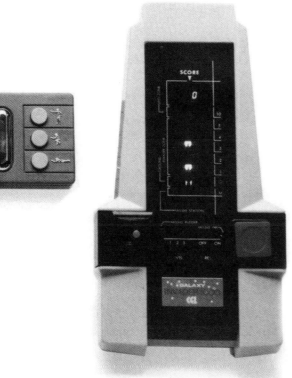

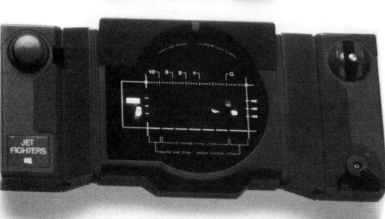

TODDLER VIDEO: THE COMPUTER AS RATTLE

Moving right down the age-scale to the infant world of pacifiers and thumbsuck cures, we come across a range of handheld video toys from Nintendo, who gave us Donkey Kong. About the size of cigarette packets, these dinky little gizmos provide simple games at two skill levels, with control buttons and jerky, Moebius strip-type screens where the action is displayed. Oh yes, and they are also alarm clocks, with a prop at the back to keep them upright: proud ornaments for any futuristic nursery.

In a sense these minigames have a stronger appeal than their more elaborate handheld cousins further up the price-range. For a start, they are self-contained conceptions working within their own limits, not just approximations of the giant consoles in the arcades. Playing a rudimentary version of Space Invaders on a calculator or a digital watch simply serves to remind you that you are not, in fact, playing

Space Invaders. Far better to make a virtue of the reduced possibilities and devise a game appropriate to the small scale.

This is what the gurus of Nintendo Inc. have come up with. In these games there are only about a dozen things that can happen: but they can happen at different speeds and in variable sequence, and in the end they provide their own peculiar satisfactions.

Two of the five games submitted to me for review owe their inspiration to legendary characters of the animated screen. In 'Popeye', Popeye sits in a little rowing-boat trying to catch various items hurled towards him by Olive Oyle. You operate his three catching positions – also avoiding Bluto, who tends to bash Popeye with

a hammer or else club him into the water with a muscular fist. In 'Mickey Mouse', Mickey Mouse has to catch eggs in a basket: there are four hens, four egg-chutes, and four catching positions. When you miss an egg it smashes and turns into a chick. You get three lives. Mickey's chick, Minnie, looks on simperingly from a barn window, but makes no visible contribution to the action. This is a neat little game which can leave you sweating with anxiety after about egg twenty-five.

Of the remaining three games, two are variations on the catching theme. In 'Chef', you have to keep tossing various items of food in the air. A grinning cat forks the odd sausage or fish; scurrying mice pick up the goodies you drop. In the more imaginative 'Parachute', you control a

GAME A

rowing-boat in a paradisal lagoon. Skydivers fall towards you, sometimes getting caught up in the palm trees where they briefly dangle before continuing their drop. If you miss them, they are horribly savaged by the shark that lurks in the blue waters. Again you have three lives – or rather the guys in the parachutes do.

A watery and violent death also awaits the competitor in 'Octopus', by some distance the best minigame on offer. Here at last the tyranny of the catching theme is resisted, though it must be admitted that the rowing-boat motif puts in another appearance. In five easy stages your helmeted patsy is obliged to descend to the depths and raid a sunken treasure chest, evading the questing tentacles of a big black octopus. If you touch any of the tentacle tips, it scoops you up and you thrash hysterically in the monster's embrace. There is a greed-factor here, since it is quite tempting to dodge about

beneath the surface pocketing the treasure and delaying your return to the boat. But the octopus turns out to be hip to this ruse – so try it at your peril.

Each unit features a Game A and a Game B, B being the speeded-up version. At both levels the contest reaches its highest pitch of difficulty quite quickly, and becomes a question of patience and concentration. After you have scored 100 points, the computer seems to lose heart; the game continues, but slackens in urgency. Because of the link-in with the timing mechanism, the games have a distinct tick-tock rhythm, a clockwork feel. This is a clear limitation, but (again) it also promotes a mesmeric quality . . . Soon Nintendo will have launched a new generation of toddlers whose first word is not 'mother' but 'microchip'. Having conquered the goo-goo market, they are no doubt buckling down to their next project: video games for the unborn.

KING OF THE CASTLE

Question: How long would it take the world's fastest computer to calculate all the possibilities of the first twenty-five moves in a game of chess?

Answer: Quite a while. Many, many times the age of the universe, to be a little more precise.

It is a flattering fact – excuse me while I examine my fingernails – that *homo sapiens* is a better chess-player than any pulsing network of spools, chips and wires. They just cannot do this stuff as well as we can. If chess is the ultimate game, then Man, for the time being, is the ultimate games-player. It won't last, but it's still nice to know.

To reduce this enigma to manageable proportions, let us take my own experience with the Mini Sensory Chess Challenger, from Fidelity Electronics Ltd., Miami, Florida. (The Mini Challenger is a pretty low-level chess computer, but then I am a pretty low-level chess human being.) In our first few games I hit the Challenger with the Queen's Gambit, in which White offers Black a pawn on the second move. If Black accepts the pawn, then White (usually) recaptures quickly and wins a slight positional advantage. Greedy, short-sighted and anal-retentive, the Challenger snapped up the pawn every time, and proceeded anxiously to defend it, with the miserably cramped QB-K3. By lazily pushing my Queen's pawn I was able, in every case, to fork Black's bishop and knight, thereby winning a piece and (in effect) the game

FIDELITY MINI SENSORY
CHESS CHALLENGER

on my fifth move. 'You don't learn, do you, dumb-dumb?' I told the Challenger. And of course the Challenger did not learn. It floundered into the same mistake every time. I gave the Challenger such a pasting – its 'I LOSE' button flashing wearily – that the machine had a nervous breakdown after 48 hours. It doesn't work any more; its lights spark and glimmer crazily if you dare to switch it on.

Not all chess computers, of course, are as easily humiliated as the wretched Challenger. Computers have been developed up to grandmaster standard and a little way beyond. The Challenger had only one idea in its tiny mind: to gain material. It had no notion of development, positioning, command of the centre, sacrifice, etc. Sophisticated machines *are* programmed to care about these things, and can naturally make much faster and more rigorous calculations than any mere Earthling. Yet a Karpov or a Korchnoi could trounce them blindfold. Why is this?

Along with music and mathematics, chess is the only human activity which produces prodigies: i.e., pre-adolescents capable of turning out creative work of the highest standard. Now, a computer can, theoretically, cope with the mathematics of chess – but not with its music. Artistic instinct lurks somewhere deep in the board's sixty-four squares, and this is something that cannot be programmed, fed in, accounted for. So tough luck! The computers will just have to sit back for a while and watch our smoke.

As for the games offered on the commercial market, it comes as no surprise that the more money you pay, the more formidable your opponent is likely to be. (The Mini Challenger is cheap, and no real challenge at all.) Also, the more advanced the machine, the longer it takes over each move. It can test the patience to watch the computer thrown into a five-minute reverie by your 1. P-K4. For my money, though, a good chess computer is an infinitely better investment than any TV plug-in Astrosmasher or handheld egg-and-spoon race console. Chess, after all, is infinite and inexhaustible, as the computers know only too well.

THE SOFT MACHINE

Everything that takes place on the screen – a Mutant attack, a powerpack munch, an asteroid cluster, plus noises, colour, manoeuvring – is simply the machine's response to *information*. The computer receives instructions from its own microprocessor, and also from the player. The player reacts to the images on the screen by manipulating his controls, which in turn react by flashing information to the microchip, which in turn (and co-instantaneously) represents this information on the screen. Got it?

All programs can be split up into separate parts, lines of instructions known as 'routines'. Take Chomp. A chunk of cake is displayed on the screen, one part of it marked 'poisoned'. The idea is to chomp the cake without eating the poisoned part: you force your opponent to eat it instead.

The first part of the program tells the computer to print the instructions on the screen at a certain position. In lines 191 to 360 it goes on storing information vital to the operation of the program memory at specific locations. From lines 390 to 430 you are asked how many players there will be and to give their names. In this routine the program is told to balk if more than nine rows are entered: it will jump back to line 420 and ask the number to be entered again. The lines up to 800 tell the computer what to print on the screen, using its special graphics characters: i.e., the picture of the cake.

On line 810 the player's name is printed and the computer asks for the co-ordinates of the square which the player wants to chomp. Note how in the following lines the program checks whether the player has entered values that are outside the game's specified range. If the player does this, line 901 tells him that he can't, and the program loops round to the beginning of the routine to ask for the values again. Now the computer displays the cake with the appropriate area chomped. Each player has his turn. At line 880 the computer discovers that the poisoned piece of cake has been duly chomped, and flashes a message to this effect on 990, along with the player's name. The computer then politely asks you if you want another game. If you do, the program jumps back to the start. If you don't, it plays a little music and says goodnight. Don't you wish you had friends like that?

The program is written for a Sharp MZ-80K computer, but can easily be adapted for other home sets.

```
8 DIM N$(10)
10 PRINT" "
20 PRINTTAB(15)::PRINT"C H O M P"
40 PRINTTAB(14)::PRINT"¯¯¯¯¯¯¯¯¯"
55 PRINT" The board is set out like a large piece"
65 PRINT" of cake,but the piece in the top right"
75 PRINT" hand corner is POISONED."
85 PRINT"     KILL your opponent by forcing him"
25 PRINT"     to take the poisoned section."
130 PRINT"     Choose the board size - up to 9x9"
150 PRINT"     The poisoned piece is shown as ▓"
160 PRINT"     edible pieces are displayed as ▓"
165 PRINT
120 PRINT"PRESS ANY KEY TO CARRY ON"
121 FOR B=1 TO 50:FOR R=255 TO 1 STEP -1:POKE4514,R:POKE4513,R:USR(68):NEXT
122 USR(71)
195 GETA$:IFA$=""THEN195
200 PRINT" "
280 DIM A(10,10)
290 PRINT" "
300 F=1
310 F=0
320 FOR I=1 TO 10
330 FOR J=1 TO 10
340 A(I,J)=0
350 NEXT J
360 NEXT I
380 PRINT" "
390 INPUT"HOW MANY PLAYERS ";P
391 FOR F=1 TO P
393 INPUT"INPUT NAMES OF PLAYERS ";N$(F)
394 NEXT
400 I1=0
410 PRINT" "
420 INPUT"HOW MANY ROWS ";R
430 IF R<=9 THEN 480
440 PRINT" "
450 PRINT"The maximum amount of columns is 9"
460 GOTO 420
470 PRINT" "
480 PRINT" "
490 INPUT"HOW MANY COLUMNS ";C:PRINT" "
500 IF C<=9 THEN 540
510 PRINT" "
520 PRINT"The maximum amount of columns is 9"
530 GOTO 490
540 PRINT"    "
550 FOR I=1 TO R
560 FOR J=1 TO C
570 A(I,J)=1
580 NEXT J
590 NEXT I
600 A(1,1)=-1
610 PRINT"  ";
620 PRINT"1 2 3 4 5 6 7 8 9"
630 FOR I=1 TO R
640 PRINT I;
650 FOR J=1 TO C
660 IF A(I,J)=-1 THEN 700
670 IF A(I,J)=0 THEN 720
680 PRINT"▓";:PRINT" ";
690 GOTO 710
700 PRINT"▓";:PRINT" ";
710 NEXT J
720 PRINT
721 FOR E=0 TO 50
722 POKE4513,E:POKE 4514,E
723 USR(68)
724 NEXT E
725 PRINT
726 USR(71)
730 NEXT I
740 PRINT
750 IF F=0 THEN 770
```

```
770 LET I1=I1+1
780 LET P1=I1-INT(I1/P)*P
790 IF P1<>0 THEN 810
800 P1=P
810 PRINT"Player ";P1
820 INPUT"Coordinates of CHOMP (Row,Column) ";R1,C1
830 IF R1<1 THEN 900
840 IF R1>R THEN 900
850 IF C1<1 THEN 900
860 IF C1>C THEN 900
870 IF A(R1,C1)=0 THEN 900
880 IF A(R1,C1)=-1 THEN 980
885 PRINT" "
890 GOTO 920
900 PRINT"                "
901 PRINT"You can't CHOMP an empty space!!      "
910 FOR D=1 TO 5000:NEXT D:GOTO 810
920 FOR I=R1 TO R
930 FOR J=C1 TO C
940 A(I,J)=0
950 NEXT J
960 NEXT I
970 GOTO 610
980 PRINT" "
990 PRINT"Bad luck you have lost player ";P1
1000 PRINT
1010 PRINT"Do you want to play again (YES OR NO) ";
1020 INPUT A$
1030 IF A$="YES" THEN 290
1035 PRINT" "
1036 PRINT"                  ";
1037 PRINT"CLOSEDOWN!!"
1040 L1$="C4C1R1C5D5.B6C3D5"
1050 L2$="E4E1R1E5F5E6D3C5"
1060 L3$="D5C5.B5C7C3R2"
1070 L4$="C3D3E3F36461R16461R16461R1"
1080 L5$="G6F3E5F4F1R1F4F1R1F4F1R1"
1090 L6$="F6E3D5E5F3E3D3C3"
2000 L7$="E6F3G6A3F3E7D7C8"
2010 TEMPO5
2020 MUSIC L1$;L2$;L3$;L4$;L5$;L6$;L7$
2025 PRINT" "
2030 FOR A=1 TO 300:R=INT(80*RND(1))
2040 S=INT(70*RND(1))
2050 SET R,S:NEXT A
2060 PRINT" "
2070 PRINT"                  ";
2080 PRINT"G O O D N I G H T ! !"
2090 FOR D=1 TO 300:NEXT D
2100 PRINT" "
2110 FOR BS=1 TO 10000:NEXT BS
2120 END
```

RUBIK'S CUBE

The working wardrobe of the standard arcade vidkid goes something like this: bobble hat, earphones, windbreaker or flying-jacket, jeans, moonboots (with perhaps some outsize rollerskates strapped on underneath) – and, of course, a Rubik's Cube keyring dangling from his belt. It is, in every sense, part of the look.

What is this passion to solve Rubik's Cube? Why do cube-solving paperbacks ride high in the bestseller lists, along with the sneaker books and self-help manuals? Why do intelligent youngsters mangle their lives in order to 'do the Cube' in twenty-five seconds? What is it with Rubik's Cube?

I don't know; and I have never talked to or read anyone who did know. But it is clearly all of a piece with the video boom. My guess is that Rubik came up with a puzzle that rides on a perfect pitch of difficulty, while somehow managing to boast a mystic simplicity at the same time. This is what levitating Nepalese monks do when they take five: they do the cube.

It's a great relief, I must say, to sit back and let the computer solve the hateful square. Another image of the video age: buy a Rubik's Cube, and feed it to your TV.

Rubik's Cube runs in 16K on a 40 column Pet

```
1 PP=0:POKE59468,12
2 PRINT"⊐⊠MAGIC CUBE SOLVER⊠"
3 PRINT"⊠⊠COPYRIGHT P.N. & M.J. RICHARDS 1981"
4 PRINT"⊠THIS PROGRAM WILL SOLVE THE MAGIC CUBE"
5 PRINT"PUZZLE FROM WHATEVER POSITION YOU ENTER"
6 PRINT"BY GIVING YOU PRECISE INSTRUCTIONS AS"
7 PRINT"TO WHICH FACES TO ROTATE."
8 PRINT"⊠SELECT ANY FACE AS TOP. LABEL THE OTHER"
9 PRINT"FACES AS SHOWN LATER AND KEEP THE CUBE"
10 PRINT"IN THIS OVERALL POSITION THROUGHOUT. IT"
11 PRINT"IS VERY USEFUL TO IDENTIFY THE FACES BY"
12 PRINT"THE COLOURS OF THEIR CENTRE SQUARES AS"
13 PRINT"THESE NEVER CHANGE."
14 PRINT"⊠THE DIRECTIONS OF ROTATION ARE GIVEN AS"
15 PRINT"IF LOOKING DOWN ON THE TOP FACE."
16 PRINT"⊠N.B. UPPER AND LOWER CASE LETTERS MAY"
17 PRINT"BE INTERCHANGED ON SOME MACHINES."
18 DIMEX(5,5,5),CX(1,4,4,5)
19 DEFFNA(X)=X-4*INT((X-1)/4)
20 DEFFNB(X)=X-(X<5ANDX>0)*(FNA(X+A-1)-X)
25 FORA=0TO5:FORB=0TO5:FORC=0TO5:EX(A,B,C)=C:NEXTC,B,A
30 FORA=0TO1:FORB=0TO4:FORC=0TO4:FORD=0TO5:CX(A,B,C,D)=D:NEXTD,C,B,A
40 F$="TESWNB"
50 DEFFNF(X)=ASC(MID$(F$,X+1,1))
60 T$="CKATRLTALRKC"
70 PRINT"⊠⊠PRESS SHIFT TO CONTINUE"
80 WAIT152,1
100 PRINT"⊐⊠NOTATION⊠"
110 PRINT"⊠TOP FACE IS LABELLED ............... ⊠T⊠"
120 PRINT"⊠BOTTOM FACE IS LABELLED ............. ⊠B⊠"
130 PRINT"⊠FRONT FACE (SOUTH) IS LABELLED ...... ⊠S⊠"
140 PRINT"⊠BACK FACE (NORTH) IS LABELLED ....... ⊠N⊠"
150 PRINT"⊠LEFT FACE (WEST) IS LABELLED ........ ⊠W⊠"
160 PRINT"⊠RIGHT FACE (EAST) IS LABELLED ....... ⊠E⊠"
170 PRINTTAB(10)"⊠_____"
```

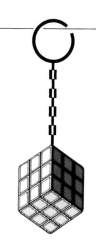

```
180 PRINTTAB(9)"/    /| N"
190 PRINTTAB(8)"/ T  / | "
200 PRINTTAB(5)"W /  / |  |"
210 PRINTTAB(7)"|‾‾‾‾|  |         ‾‾‾‾‾‾‾‾‾‾‾‾"
220 PRINTTAB(7)"|    | E |         PRESS SHIFT"
225 PRINTTAB(7)"| S  | /"          TO CONTINUE"
230 PRINTTAB(7)"|    | /"
240 PRINTTAB(7)"|____|/    "
250 WAIT152,1
255 POKE59468,14
260 PRINT"...     ...    ..."
261 PRINT"...  180... (.../ ....) ...... ...    2"
265 PRINT"...   .../  o  ..."
270 PRINT"...  90... |  o ...  . ...... ...    T"
271 PRINT"...  90... .o. | ... .  . ...... ...    A"
280 PRINT"...  / ... .  ..."
281 PRINT"...  90... |  |  |  L  | ...... ...    L"
282 PRINT"...  90... |  |  | ... | || ...... ...    R"
290 PRINT"...  | .../  | ... ..."
291 PRINT"...  90... ..'o..  ........ ...    2"
292 PRINT"...  90... ./.. ..''o... . .... ...    <"
300 PRINT"...  .. .... | .. ... ..."
301 WAIT152,1
310 PRINT"...  ...    ...    ..."
320 PRINT"... 2 .../. | / | ... | || | 180..."
330 PRINT"...A ./. | / ... ... 90... .o. | ...  ./"
340 PRINT".../L ./. | / ... ... 90... |  |  | L .|"
350 PRINT"...|K ./. | / | ... ... 90... ./.. ..''o.."
355 PRINT"..."
360 PRINT"...o.LL  ./ o./ |  | .. ./ | | | ../ ./"
370 PRINT"|  .  ..// | .. ( V/)? "
371 POKE144,50
374 GETA$:IFA$=""THEN374
375 POKE144,46:IFA$<>"Y"THENPRINT"./":GOTO377
376 PRINT" .":PP=1:OPEN4,4:PRINT#4
377 FORJ=1TO500:NEXT:PRINT"":POKE59468,12
378 A=3
379 FORL=0TO5
380 PRINT"LOOK AT THE "CHR$(FNF(L))"-FACE OF YOUR CUBE"
390 PRINT""TAB(18);CHR$(FNF(-4*(L=0ORL=5)))
400 PRINT""TAB(12)" ‾‾‾‾‾‾‾‾‾‾‾"
410 FORZ=1TO3
420 PRINTTAB(12)"|   |   |   |"
425 PRINTTAB(12)"|   |   |   |"
430 PRINTTAB(12)"|   |   |   |"
435 IFZ=3THEN460
440 PRINTTAB(12)"|---+---+---|"
450 NEXTZ
460 PRINTTAB(12)"|___|___|___|"
470 PRINT""TAB(18);CHR$(FNF(5+3*(L=0ORL=5)))
480 POKE33178,FNF(FNA(L+1+2*(L=0)+(L=5)))-64
490 POKE33194,FNF(FNA(L-1-2*(L=0)+(L=5)))-64
500 PRINT"TYPE LETTER OF FACE WHICH HAS THE SAME"
505 PRINT"COLOUR CENTRE SQUARE AS FLASHING SQUARE"
510 PRINT"(PRESS DELETE TO ERASE ANY ERROR)."
512 PRINT"PRESS RETURN WHEN  -FACE IS COMPLETE."
513 POKE33706,PEEK(32780)-128
515 PRINT""TAB(11);
```

```
520 FORY=0TO3:FORV=0TO2
530 PRINT"▓▒▒▒";
531 IFY=3THEN535
532 IFY=1ANDV=1THENA$=CHR$(PEEK(32780)-64):GOTO600
533 POKE144,50
535 GETA$:IFA$=""THEN535
536 POKE144,46
537 IFA$<>CHR$(20)THEN575
540 IFVTHEN550
545 IFY=0THEN533
546 Y=Y-1:V=2
547 PRINT" ":PRINT"▚▒▒▒▒"TAB(22);" ▐▌";:GOTO533
550 PRINT" ▐▌▌▌▌▌ ▐▌";
560 V=V-1
565 IFV=1ANDY=1THEN550
570 GOTO533
575 Q=10
577 IFY<3THEN580
578 IFASC(A$)=13THEN535
579 GOTO820
580 FORI=0TO5:IFASC(A$)=FNF(I)THENQ=I
590 NEXTI:IFQ=10THEN530
600 PRINTA$;
610 IF(Y+V)<>2*INT((Y+V)/2)THEN740
620 IFY=1THEN800
625 IFL=0ORL=5THEN660
630 T=-(Y=2)
640 J=FNA(L-V+1):K=L
650 GOTO710
660 T=L/5
670 J=FNA(V-1-2*(L=5)):K=4-Y
710 C%(T,J,K,L)=Q
720 C%(T,K,J,L)=Q
730 GOTO800
740 IFY-1THENK=32866+Y*320
750 IFY=1THENK=33178+V*8
760 FORX=0TO5:IFPEEK(K)+64=FNF(X)THENE%(X,L,L)=Q:E%(L,X,L)=Q
770 NEXTX
800 NEXTV
810 PRINT:PRINT"▚▒▒▒"TAB(11);:NEXTY
820 NEXTL
825 POKE59468,14
830 PRINT"▚▚▞▖▛▀▀▀▘o │ ▐▜▀ ╲▞♦│▁▁▖╲▞♦▘▁▀▆"
840 PRINT"▚▌▐▀ ▃♦▁▀▁▖▖▐▔▌ ▐▔ ♠▌▐▀▔▁ │ ▐▔ ▀♦▖▁▞♦   ▀▁ │ ▐▔ ▃♦▀▔♦ ▁ ▖▘▀▀▔▀▔ │ ▐╱
▀▔▁▗"
850 PRINT
1000 A=0:FORB=1TO4
1010 FORR=0TO5:FORS=0TO5
1020 IFE%(R,S,R)=0THENIFE%(R,S,S)=BTHENE=R:F=S
1030 NEXT:NEXT
1037 IFE=FNA(E)ANDF=FNA(F)THEN1065
1038 IFE+F<5THEN1048
1039 BR=FNA(E+F-B)-1
1040 ONBR+1GOTO1048,1041,1042,1043
1041 M$="B":GOTO1045
1042 M$="B2":GOTO1045
1043 M$="B-1"
1045 GOSUB5000
```

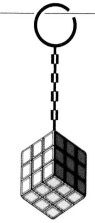

```
1046  IFF=5THENE=B:GOTO1048
1047  F=B
1048  IFE=0ANDF=BTHEN1140
1049  A=E+F+5*(E+F>5):M$="E":GOSUB5000
1050  IFE=FNA(E)THENF=FNA(E+INT(F/2)-1):GOTO1065
1060  E=FNA(F+INT(E/2)-1)
1065  QQ=0
1070  TR=FNA(F-B+1)-1
1075  ONTR+1GOTO1096,1080,1085,1090
1080  M$="T":GOTO1095
1085  M$="T2":GOTO1095
1090  M$="T-1"
1095  GOSUB5000
1096  IFQQ=1THEN1140
1097  A=F
1100  IFFNA(E-F)=1THENM$="E":GOTO1120
1110  M$="E-1"
1120  GOSUB5000
1130  QQ=1:TR=4-TR+4*(TR=0):GOTO1075
1140  NEXTB
1150  FORB=1TO4
1160  FORTB=0TO1:FORS=1TO4
1170  R=FNA(S-1)
1180  F1=C%(TB,S,R,5*TB)
1190  F2=C%(TB,S,R,S)
1200  F3=C%(TB,S,R,R)
1210  IFF1*F2*F3THEN1230
1220  IFF1*F1+F2*F2+F3*F3=B*B+FNA(B-1)↑2THENE=TB:F=S
1230  NEXTS,TB
1232  IFE=0ANDF=BANDC%(0,F,FNA(F-1),0)=0THEN1370
1240  IFETHEN1280
1250  A=F
1260  M$="EBE-1":GOSUB5000
1270  F=FNA(F-1)
1280  BR=FNA(F-B+1)-1
1290  ONBR+1GOTO1340,1300,1310,1320
1300  M$="B":GOTO1330
1310  M$="B2":GOTO1330
1320  M$="B-1"
1330  GOSUB5000
1340  A=B:IFC%(1,B,FNA(B-1),FNA(B-1))=0THENM$="N-1B-1N":GOSUB5000:GOTO1370
1350  IFC%(1,B,FNA(B-1),5)=0THENM$="EB2E-1B-1":GOSUB5000
1360  M$="EBE-1":GOSUB5000
1370  NEXTB
1375  D$="B-1E-1BEBSB-1S-1"
1380  FORB=1TO4
1390  FORR=1TO5:FORS=1TO5
1400  IFEX%(R,S,R)=BTHENIFEX%(R,S,S)=FNA(B-1)THENE=R:F=S
1410  NEXT:NEXT
1420  IFE=BANDF=FNA(B-1)THEN1590
1430  IFE=5ORF=5THEN1470
1435  IFF=FNA(E+1)THENA=E:GOTO1450
1440  A=F
1450  M$=D$:GOSUB5000
1460  GOTO1390
1470  IFE=5THENQ=F:GOTO1485
1480  Q=E
1485  GT=EX%(E,F,Q)
```

```
1490  BR=FNA(E+F-GT)-1
1500  ONBR+1GOTO1550,1510,1520,1530
1510  M$="B":GOTO1540
1520  M$="B2":GOTO1540
1530  M$="B-1"
1540  GOSUB5000
1550  A=FNA(GT-1)
1560  IFGT=BTHENM$=D$:GOTO1580
1570  M$="BWB-1W-1B-1S-1BS"
1580  GOSUB5000
1590  NEXTB
1600  R=0:FORB=1TO4
1610  BB=FNA(B-1)
1615  J(B)=0
1620  IFC%(1,B,BB,B)*C%(1,B,BB,BB)*C%(1,B,BB,5)=5*B*BBTHENJ(B)=1:R=R+1
1630  NEXT
1640  ONR+1GOTO1655,1680,1650,0,1750
1650  IFJ(1)=J(3)THEN1660
1655  M$="B":GOSUB5000:GOTO1600
1660  A=2-J(2)
1670  M$="BSWBW-1B-1S-1":GOSUB5000:GOTO1600
1680  FORB=1TO4:IFJ(B)=1THENA=B
1690  NEXT
1700  S=C%(1,A,FNA(A+1),5)*C%(1,A,FNA(A+1),A)*C%(1,A,FNA(A+1),FNA(A+1))
1710  IFS=5*A*FNA(A-1)THENM$="W-1BEB-1WBE-1B-1":GOTO1730
1720  M$="BEB-1W-1BE-1B-1W"
1730  GOSUB5000:GOTO1600
1750  R=0:FORB=1TO4
1755  BB=FNA(B-1)
1760  J(B)=0
1770  IFC%(1,B,BB,5)=5THENJ(B)=1:R=R+1
1780  NEXT
1790  ONR+1GOTO1850,1830,1800,0,1900
1800  IFJ(1)=J(3)THEN1820
1810  A=J(4)*2+J(3)-J(4)*(J(3)*2-1)+1:GOTO1860
1820  A=J(3)+1:GOTO1860
1830  FORB=1TO4:IFJ(B)=1THENA=FNA(B-1)
1840  NEXT:GOTO1860
1850  A=3
1860  IFC%(1,FNB(3),FNB(2),FNB(2))=5THENM$="W-1TWSTS-1BST-1S-1W-1T-1WB-1":GOTO1880
1870  M$="BW-1TWSTS-1B-1ST-1S-1W-1T-1W"
1880  GOSUB5000:GOTO1750
1900  R=0:A=3:FORB=1TO4
1920  IFE%(5,B,5)*E%(5,B,B)=5*BTHENA=B:R=R+1
1930  NEXT
1940  ONR+1GOTO1970,1960,0,0,2000
1960  IFE%(5,FNB(2),FNB(2))*E%(5,FNB(2),5)=5*FNB(4)THENM$="W2BSN-1W2NS-1BW2":GOTO1980
1970  M$="W2B-1SN-1W2NS-1B-1W2"
1980  GOSUB5000:GOTO1900
2000  R=0:A=2:FORB=1TO4
2010  J(B)=0
2020  IFE%(5,B,5)=5THENJ(B)=1:R=R+1
2030  NEXT
2040  ONR+1GOTO2080,0,2050,0,3000
2050  IFJ(1)=J(3)THEN2070
2060  A=J(3)*2+J(2)-J(3)*(J(2)*2-1)+1:M$="SBT-1E2B2T2WBW-1T2B2E2TB-1S-1B-1":GOTO2090
```

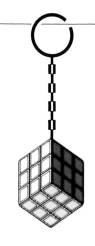

```
2070 A=2-J(1)
2080 M$="SBT-1E2B2T2WB2W-1T2B2E2TB-1S-1B2"
2090 GOSUB5000:GOTO2000
3000 IFEE=120REE=25THENPRINT:IFPP=1THENPRINT#4
3005 PRINT"🔲-\-/-◆":IFPP=1THENPRINT#4,"🔲FINIS":CLOSE4
4900 END
5000 IFM$=""THENRETURN
5010 R$=LEFT$(M$,1)
5015 IFR$=M$THEN5030
5020 IFASC(MID$(M$,2))<64THENR$=LEFT$(M$,12-ASC(MID$(M$,2))/5)
5030 M$=MID$(M$,LEN(R$)+1)
5040 FORU=0TO5:IFASC(R$)=FNF(U)THENL=FNB(U)
5050 NEXTU
5054 IFPP=1THENPRINT#4,"🔲"CHR$(FNF(L));
5055 PRINTCHR$(FNF(L)+128);
5056 EE=EE+1
5057 IFLEN(R$)=2THENSF$="2  ":GOTO5059
5058 SF$=MID$(T$,L*2+1+LEN(R$)/2,1)+"  "
5059 PRINTSF$;:IFPP=1THENPRINT#4,"🔲"SF$;
5061 IFEE=13THENPRINT:IFPP=1THENPRINT#4
5062 IFEE=26THENPRINT"🔲":EE=0:IFPP=1THENPRINT#4:PRINT#4
5065 FORLP=1TOLEN(R$)
5070 A(0)=-4*(L=0ORL=5):A(4)=A(0)
5080 A(1)=FNA(L-1-2*(L=0)+(L=5))
5090 A(2)=5+3*(L=0ORL=5)
5100 A(3)=FNA(L+1+2*(L=0)+(L=5))
5105 FORLK=0TO4:B(LK)=A(LK):NEXT
5112 E1=EX(L,A(3),L)
5114 E2=EX(L,A(3),A(3))
5120 FORTN=3TO1STEP-1
5130 EX(L,A(TN),L)=EX(L,A(TN-1),L)
5140 EX(L,A(TN),A(TN))=EX(L,A(TN-1),A(TN-1))
5150 EX(A(TN),L,A(TN))=EX(A(TN-1),L,A(TN-1))
5160 EX(A(TN),L,L)=EX(A(TN-1),L,L)
5170 NEXTTN
5175 EX(L,A(0),L)=E1:EX(A(0),L,L)=E1
5180 EX(L,A(0),A(0))=E2:EX(A(0),L,A(0))=E2
5190 IFL>0ANDL<5THENA(0)=L:A(4)=L:A(2)=L
5200 T=-(L=5)
5210 C1=C%(T,A(3),A(0),L)
5215 C2=C%(T,A(3),A(0),B(3))
5220 C3=C%(T,A(3),A(0),B(0))
5230 FORTN=3TO1STEP-1
5240 T1=-((TN<3ANDL>0)ORL=5)
5250 T2=-((TN>1ANDL>0)ORL=5)
5260 C%(T1,A(TN+1),A(TN),L)=C%(T2,A(TN),A(TN-1),L)
5270 C%(T1,A(TN),A(TN+1),L)=C%(T2,A(TN-1),A(TN),L)
5280 C%(T1,A(TN+1),A(TN),B(TN))=C%(T2,A(TN),A(TN-1),B(TN-1))
5290 C%(T1,A(TN),A(TN+1),B(TN))=C%(T2,A(TN-1),A(TN),B(TN-1))
5300 C%(T1,A(TN),A(TN+1),B(TN+1))=C%(T2,A(TN-1),A(TN),B(TN))
5310 C%(T1,A(TN+1),A(TN),B(TN+1))=C%(T2,A(TN),A(TN-1),B(TN))
5320 NEXTTN
5330 C%(T,A(0),A(1),L)=C1:C%(T,A(1),A(0),L)=C1
5340 C%(T,A(0),A(1),B(0))=C2:C%(T,A(1),A(0),B(0))=C2
5350 C%(T,A(0),A(1),B(1))=C3:C%(T,A(1),A(0),B(1))=C3
5360 NEXTLP
5370 GOTO5000
READY.
```

THE SPACE RACE: VIDEO COMPETITIONS

'Wanna play two?' is the average arcade-loner's introduction to the world of video competition. You turn from the screen to find a hungry-looking individual with his twenty pee poised and an expression on his face ranging from wistfulness to candid desperation. You put your money in the slot; he puts his money in the slot; you press the Two-Player button rather than the One-Player: this is amateur video competition, as practised throughout the land, indeed throughout the globe. It is an arcade convention, and a good one – simply a way of getting new players on the machine with a minimum of bloodshed. This is an old tradition in pinball praxis (nowadays most pinball machines are equipped to accommodate four simultaneous players), which has carried over into video. You may glance at your playmate's score from time to time, you may occasionally murmur 'Nice' or 'Unlucky' or 'Smart Bomb!' or 'Hyperspace!' – and you certainly compare high scores with your friends and arcade

STEVE DAVIS PRESENTING THE WINNER OF *COMPUTER AND VIDEO GAMES'* 'BEST ARCADE PLAYER' COMPETITION, PETER EDMONDS, WITH HIS ROSETTE.

acquaintances – but really you're just champing to get back on the console.

The world of organized video competition is something else again. Basically these space rallies are PR-fests, all logo T-shirts, holiday-camp

THE BBC'S 'SPACE INVADER OF THE MIDLANDS' COMPETITION: TOYAH PICTURED WITH THE WINNER, ROD WILLIAMS (14) OF WALSALL.

ATLANTA ASTEROIDS VIDEO CONTEST

bonhomie and heavy-jawed corporation high-ups fretting about the company image. Here is an imaginary but typical scenario, a press release straight from the land of fancy:

In Nowhere, Nebraska, last week Dyslexia Leisure Systems Inc. launched their latest space game, Splurk, with an all-comers mixed-singles championship in the city's new Blastfurter Entertainments Metroplex. Fourteen-year-old John Stircrazy ran out clear winner with a score of well over five squillion points. Awarding young John his Splurk T-shirt and ultra-violet eyeshade, Dyslexia Inc.'s sales-manager Flip Boyland had this to say about the competition's success: 'We are all very encouraged by the response these young people have shown to Dyslexia's new product. We certainly hope that . . .' Etcetera, etcetera.

The artificiality of this kind of space race has another aspect. The top video athletes can stay on a machine more or less indefinitely. Taking bites of proffered pizza between each wave, slurping coke through a six-foot straw, and boasting bladders the size of Oklahoma, the crack vidkids have been known to play for over sixty hours non-stop. You hear of Asteroids experts abandoning a game with a score of ten million and with fifteen lives left on the clock; perhaps they just faint away. Clearly no sponsored competition could be run a along these lines — think of all the Negative Publicity from distraught mothers, missing-persons operatives, and so on. Instead, there is a time limit — often as low as fifteen minutes — and the contestants win their logo-ed sneakers and bobble-hats simply by scoring against the clock.

The space games are competitive all right; but the competitive spirit they appeal to is more abstract than the stopwatch frenzy which these contests seek to exploit. Me, I don't even like playing two-up; nor do I enjoy having some arcade humanoid going cold turkey over my shoulder when I'm busy defending Earth. The true video addict just wants to be left alone with his machine. In a sense, he is competing against the software, the logic board. But the machine doesn't mind if you beat it — and you never can beat it, not in the end, not really. Who does mind? You do. As always, *homo ludens* is ultimately competing against himself.

WHO'S WHO IN THE ALIEN WORLD?

'I'd know that space-face anywhere . . .' Oh yeah? It is time to take a stroll down the cosmic ID parade. 'That was the one, officer – *he* did it.' But you'd better get it right. Finger the wrong Space Invader, and his galactic pals will come knocking on your door.

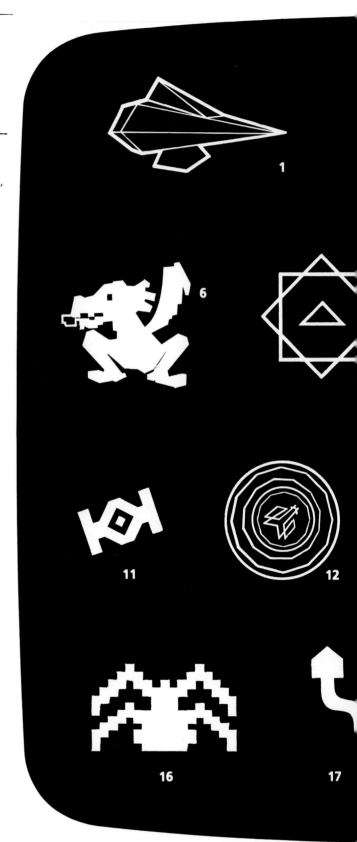

Answers on page 127

3

4

5

8

9

10

13

14

15

18

19

20

GLOSSARY

A Guide to Arcade Argot – Also to Some Trans-Atlantic Ambiguities

ace – video-game expert

alky – alcoholic

automated extremity – robot arm

bad boulder – boulder containing enemies in Asteroids de Luxe

Basic – the language spoken by home computers

bits – binary digits

bleeding – what happens to supernumerary elements on overloaded screen; they bleed to another quadrant

bleeping sickness – nightmares brought about by playing too much video

bottling out – chickening out

bug – computer hitch

cart – video cartridge

chip – small piece of silicon, holding all components of a microprocessor

Command Mission – most difficult mission in Lunar Lander

Concorde – valuable enemy ship in Galaxian

counting – technique in Space Invaders; you count shots to score extra points on Saucers

dedicated – not able to be reprogrammed

diamond bomb – rhomboid grenade in Missile Command

dog – bad machine

Domestos – disinfectant that 'kills all known germs'

fag – cigarette

faggot – gay

Fatboy – big saucer in Asteroids

frust – thrust

gosub – command instructing computer to go to a subroutine

graphics characters – pictorial representation of data

hardware – the actual machine

humanoid – power-pack in Defender; also someone who hangs around arcades

hyperspace – warping to another quadrant

Invadee – video addict

kilobyte – measurement of memory capacity: 1,024 bytes

learning the board – getting the hang of a machine

lemon – the muncher in PacMan

logic board – software

loop – repeated execution of series of instructions

lurking – technique in Asteroids; you hang around waiting for Pimples (NB: not possible in Asteroids de Luxe: Pimple's first photon will destroy last boulder)

microworld – autonomous world of individual computer

munching – point-eating in PacMan

Mutant – squealing alien in Defender; also video addict

nick – maintenance level of machine; in good nick = in good shape

Pimple – small saucer in Asteroids

photon – little white bomb

poke – instruction allowing you to store integers in a specific place in memory

poodle – bad machine

punter – video-game player

rack – wave or 'sheet' of aliens

routine – sub-set of coded instructions

scam – tricking the computer

scanner – radar console in Defender

sheet – see rack

smart bomb – bomb that kills everything on screen

soaksite – test site for video game

software – the program fed into the computer

Space Avenger – highest rank in Gorf

Triffid – video addict

tweak – clinching gimmick for new machine; the come-on

value – numerical quantity of a data element

vidkid – young video addict

warping – going into hyperspace; also (colloq.) leaving, as in 'I warped out of the pizza parlour'

wraparound – capability of leaving screen and coming back the other side

zembla – reformed video addict

ACKNOWLEDGEMENTS

We wish to thank the following for providing photographs and illustrations for reproduction:

Ace Ltd, pages 98 *below* and 99;
Activision/John Morrison Communications, 99 *centre*;
Atari UK Ltd, 98 *above* and 102;
BBC Midlands, 120 *below*;
Mick Brownfield, front cover;
David Cockcroft, 45 and 68–9 *below*;
Computer and Video Games Magazine, 120 *above*;
Paul Davies, 27;
Phil Dobson, 11, 12 and back jacket;
Jeremy Enness, 18–19, 20 *above* and *below*, 21 *centre left*, *below left* and *below right*, 24 *centre left* and *below left*, 25 *below*, 28 *above* and *below*, 29, 57 *above*, 100, 106–7, 109 *below* and 110;
Gamma, pages 13 *above*, 24 *above*, 31, 104 *below*, 105, 112 and 121;
Val Hill, 111 and 113;
Su Huntley, 17;
Bob Layzell/Young Artists, 71 and 72;
Angus McKie/Young Artists, 54;
Mattel Electronics, 97 and 103;
Midway Manufacturing Co., 51 *right*;
NAP Consumer Electronics Corporation, 96 and 101;
Kevin O'Keefe, 95;
Philips Videopac, 101 *inset*;
Red Saunders, 13 *below*, 22, 23 *above right* and *centre right*, 24 *below right*, 30, 38, 41, 42–3 and 88–9;
Sega/Gremlin, 84 and 85;
Sunday Times Magazine, photo by Red Saunders, 23 *below right*;
Sygma, photo by Jim McHugh, 6;
Transworld Features, photos by Dan McCoy, 8–9, 21 *above*, 32, 33, 34 and 35 *above* and *below*;
USICA/NASA, 67 *below*;
J and J Walker/Valian Studios, 90, 91, 92 and 93 *above*;
Alan Watson Studio, 14–15.

Video-screen diagrams by John Thompson and Baxter & Knopp Associates.

Additional illustrations and photographs are by David Brown, Val Hill and Harry Wilson.

Grateful thanks are also due to The Crystal Room, Brighton, Victor Lownes, Ruffler & Deith and The Venue, Victoria for permission to photograph on their premises.

All the video games featured in this book are trademarked by their manufacturers:
Asteroids, Asteroids de Luxe, Battlezone, Centipede, Lunar Lander, Missile Command and Tempest – *Atari, Inc.*
Pleiads – *Centuri, Inc.*
Pro-Golf – *Data East, Inc.*
Video Hustler – *Kuonami, Inc.*
Galaxian, Gorf and PacMan – *Midway Manufacturing Co.*
Dribbling – *Model Racing.*
Donkey Kong – *Nintendo Leisure System Co. Ltd.*
Scramble – *Stern Electronics, Inc.*
Frogger and Turbo – *Sega/Gremlin.*
Space Invader and Space Invaders Part II, etc. – *Taito Electronics Ltd.*
Cosmic Alien – *Universal, Inc.*
Defender – *Williams Electronics, Inc.*

Inclusion of the products of any of the above-named manufacturers in no way implies their endorsement of any of the views expressed in the text.

Thanks are also due to Terry Brown for the Chomp program, Matthew Richards for the Rubik's Cube program, and to Bruce Nicholson for technical advice.

Quiz answers
1 Battlezone; 2 Gorf; 3 Space Invaders II;
4 Galaxian; 5 Missile Command; 6 Wizard of Wor; 7 Omega Race; 8 Pleiads; 9 Asteroids;
10 Scramble; 11 Astro Fighter; 12 Star Castle;
13 Defender; 14 Tempest; 15 Phoenix;
16 Centipede; 17 Venture; 18 Astro Blaster;
19 Berzerk; 20 Red Baron.

"WELL DONE EARTHLINGS-
NEXT TIME YOU WIN"